Air Pistol Target Shooting

Dr. Baljit Singh Sekhon
Deputy Director of Sports & Head,
Nagaland University,
Kohima (Nagaland)

SPORTS PUBLICATION

7/26, Ground Floor, Ansari Road,
Darya Ganj, New Delhi-110002
Phones: (Office) 65749511 (Fax) 011-23240261
(Mobile) 9868028838 (Residence) 27562163
E-mail: lakshaythani@hotmail.com

Published by:

SPORTS PUBLICATION
7/26, Ground Floor, Ansari Road, Darya Ganj, New Delhi-110002
Ph. : (Office) 65749511, 23240261 (Mobile) 9868028838
    (Residence) 27562163 (Fax) 011-23240261
E-mail: *lakshaythani@hotmail.com*

© 2009 Publishers

I.S.B.N: 978-81-7879-550-8

PRINTED IN INDIA 2009

All Rights Reserved

No part of this publication may be stored in a retrieval system, transmitted, or reproduced in any way, including but not limited to photocopy, photograph, magnetic or other record, without the prior agreement and written permission of the publisher.

Laser Typeset by:
JAIN MEDIA GRAPHICS,
C-4/95-A, Keshav Puram, Delhi-35

Printed by:
CHAWLA OFFSET PRINTERS, Delhi-110052

Price: Rs. 395/-

Preface

I am honoured to have been asked to write the Foreword to this book. Improving performance is a goal that requires constant effort by the both shooters and coaches. This book is our response to the many queries we receive at the beginning level of shooting. It is intended to be the first volume in a long series that will bring state of the art information to the Indian Shooting Community.

The *"Air Pistol Target Shooting"* written by Dr. Baljit Singh Sekhon is based on his thirteen years of experience in shooting sports. He is one of the coaches who have been able to glean the true fundamentals of marksmanship, separating them from techniques and legend fundamentals necessary to make a good shot.

The topics he has covered are wide in scope and range, which include three numerous chapters. The first chapter analyses the retrospective study of shooting sports, safety requirements, equipments and accessories. This chapter consists of learned topics dealing with various aspects of general pistol shooting. The second chapter contains valuable comments on the basic shooting skills, which are essential for good shooting-stance, grip, aiming, breath control, trigger release and follow through. The third chapter is comprehensive and detailed with important topics like anatomy, physiology, fitness, training, psychology, drugs in shooting sports and nutrition. This chapter is an account of the appended fields of shooting followed by expert glossary.

I hope that the information in this book will help to meet your information requirements in order to improve your shooting performances. This volume will give the reader a greater insight into air pistol shooting. On the whole this book is a scholarly study of some of the important facets of pistol shooting. I personally hope the publishing of this book will render great service to the shooters and will enhance shooting culture among the people in various parts of the nation. I wish the book and the author all success.

Donald William
USA

NAGALAND UNIVERSITY

℡ (0370) 2290488 (O)
(0370) 2242701 (R)
Fax : (0370) 2230349 (O)
Gram : Nagavarsity
Email : vicechancellornu@yahoo.com
Website: www.nagauniv.org.in

(Headquarters : Lumami)
Kohima Campus, Kohima - 797 001
Nagaland, India.

Prof. K. Kannan
Vice Chancellor

FORWARD

It gives me an immense pleasure in writing the forward to the book *"Air Pistol Target Shooting"* by Dr Baljit Singh Sekhon, Deputy Director of Sports, Nagaland University.

As Sport academicians take the trouble to write down their understanding, experiences and pitfalls within their profession, be it any field, can help in the furtherance of knowledge and wisdom and not reinvent the wheel. This will allow the trainer to provide quality training and discipline to prospective medal winners. In spite of such books, Mr. Bindra by his own commitment with support from his presents, made India proud by winning Gold against very stiff competitors.

I hope this book will not only inspire the youth to take up Air Pistol Shooting but bring laurel to themselves and the country. I hope the book will be regularly updated so that it will make our youth competitive in this area.

With Best wishes to all who will take the trouble of not only reading but practicing the tips provided.

Prof. K. Kannan

Acknowledgements

The process of writing this book began around the end of December 2004, when I landed in New Delhi after my participation at the "International Shooting Sports Federation", (Germany) Judge and Jury "B" Course. During my interaction with various leading personalities at the course, I discovered that it is one's own view comparable and adaptable at the literature. The outcome of this modest though process is the present book.

This is the time when NRAI is celebrating the Golden Jubilee of the National Shooting Championship Competition (NSCC) and it is also an auspicious occasion as we celebrate the Indian shooters who have made proud of our country by winning a number of medals in World Championships, World Cups, Asian Games and Commonwealth Games, especially one Gold Medal in Beijing Olympics by Abhinav Bindra and one silver medal in Athens Olympics by Lt. Gol. R.V.S. Rathore. A number of famous shooters have been brought forth through National Rifle Association of India, which is one of the best managed sports federation in the country.

I am sincerely indebted to National Rifle Association of India and so also Sh. Baljit Singh Sethi, Secretary General of N.R.A.I. for enabling me to attend the course.

AIR PISTOL TARGET SHOOTING

His continued encouragement and a reassuring attitude, without whose enthusiasm, this book would not have seen the light of the day.

I take pleasure to express my thanks to those whose brains have been ruthlessly plundered during the entire period of my research. I specially acknowledge the painstaking efforts made by Mr. Donald William, Shooting Coach, USA and Mrs. Sarah Daly, U.K. in giving a cogent shape to the intricate part of the text. My sincere thanks are also due to Prof. Sunny Thomas, National Coach, Mr. Laszlo Szuchack, Rifle Coach, Mr. Tibor Gonczel, Pistol Coach and Col. Jaswant Singh, for contributing their professional expertise in developing some of the concept dwelt upon in this book.

I also thank Mr. T.S. Dhillon, Mr. Rajiv Bhatia, Mr. R. Choudhary, Mr. Daleep Chandel, Mr. Randhir Singh, Dr. S.K. Dhillon, Dr. Sukhdev Singh, Sh. Raja Sidhu, Sh. N.S. Bhogal and Sh. Ajit Singh for their interest in my academic activities and Sh. Santokh Singh, Sh. Avtar Singh, for their consistent help in providing me the necessary information and support.

My thanks with gratitude are due to Shri P. Zetsuvi and my parents for their precious support in carrying out this task. I will be falling in my duty if I don't express my profound gratitude to my friend Jagdip Singh Lally for his invaluable suggestions and assistance in this study. I also indebted and feel deep appreciation for my wife for her co-operation, who supported me for accomplishing this task.

AIR PISTOL TARGET SHOOTING

I am indebted to Prof. (Dr.) K. Kannan, Vice-Chancellor and Shri T. Vihienuo, Registrar of Nagaland University for giving me ample encouragement for publish this book.

(Dr. Baljit Singh Sekhon)
Deputy Director of Sports and Head
Nagaland University, Kohima

Contents

Preface	iii
Foreword	v
Acknowledgements	vi

CHAPTER I   **1-27**

INTRODUCTION	1
1. THE HISTORY OF SHOOTING	6
a. Development of the Air Pistol	11
2. SAFETY REQUIREMENTS	15
3. EQUIPMENTS AND ACCESSORIES	18
a. Pistol	19
b. Trigger	20
c. Sights	20
d. Grip	21
e. Corrective lenses and shooting glasses	21
f. Hearing Protection	22
g. Note Book	23
h. Stop Watch	23

AIR PISTOL TARGET SHOOTING

    i. Shooting Cap   24

    j. Electronic scoring Target   24

    k. Miscellaneous equipments   24

4. DOMINANT EYE   24

    a. Miller Cone Test   26

CHAPTER II   28-48

ESSENTIALS OF GOOD SHOOTING SKILLS   28

1. STANCE   28

2. THE GRIP   33

3. AIMING   35

    a. Sight Picture   36

    b. Relationship of Sight   38

4. BREATHING   42

5. TRIGGER RELEASE AND FOLLOW THROUGH   44

    a. Trigger Finger   46

    b. Follow Through   47

CHAPTER III   49-98

APPENDED FIELDS OF SHOOTING   49

1. ANATOMY AND PHYSIOLOGY   49

    a. Skeletal System   50

    b. Muscles that move the upper extremities   51

    d. Nervous System   57

AIR PISTOL TARGET SHOOTING

e. Vision	63
2. PHYSICAL FITNESS AND TRAINING	65
a. Mental Training	69
b. Strength and Isometric Training	69
c. Dry Firing	71
d. General Fitness	73
3. PSYCHOLOGY IN SHOOTING SPORTS	78
a. Motivation	80
b. Concentration	81
c. Relaxation	83
d. Attention	84
e. Autogenous Training	85
4. NUTRITION	86
a. Carbohydrates	87
b. Protein	88
c. Fats	89
d. Vitamins	89
e. Minerals	91
f. Diet before Competition	91
g. Diet during Activity	92
h. Diet after Activity	93
5. DRUGS IN SHOOTING SPORTS	94

AIR PISTOL TARGET SHOOTING

a. Alcohol — 94
b. Stimulants — 95
c. Smoking — 95
6. FIRST AID AND CORRECTIVE LENSES — 96

Glossary of the Terms — 99-114
References — 115-123

1

Introduction

The widely held thought that tends to connect shooting with aggressive manners is totally mistaken. An edgy and aggressive individual has no chance of success in shooting. On the contrary, the shooting sport demands calmness and concentration combined with physical fitness and stamina. The basic philosophy of shooting relies on the concept of "quest for perfection".

Competing in accurate shooting has a history almost as old as weaponry itself. During the 19th century, shooters began to organize themselves nationally, and one of these was French pistol champion Pierre de Coubertin, founder of the modern Olympics. Soon world championships were being organized as well. During the years, the sports have changed a number of times and new things have been added. For instance, from the beginning, many of the targets had human-like (or in the case of running target, animal-like) shapes; most have now assumed a circular form to reduce the connotations with the use of guns in wars. As for as participation is concerned however, shooting sports is one of the largest in the world.

Recently, a number of threats to the shooting sports have been revealed. One such threat is scepticism from the public, often unaware of the rigorous safety rules that surround. Therefore, this sport is falling under the extremely restrictive gun policy of some governments. Shooting requires a high degree of concentration, coordination and determination and at the same time is an enjoyable sport in which people of all ages can take part. Although compared to some sports, pistol-shooting equipments appear to be fairly technical, the sport itself is not; it is a sport of the mind and body just like any other sport.

Shooting is a learned skill that is developed through physical and psychological practice. It is the individual's desire, dedication and persistence that largely determine how successful a competitive shooter might become rather than one's own natural ability. Shooting sport is somewhat distinctive from many sporty activities in that a specific body conformation or strength is not requisite. World-class shooters are of all shapes, size and ages. So many shooters in the quest for improvement seek the erroneous way of only added equipment. But the only way to improve scores is through training of mind and body and no amount of advanced equipments, will make a worth-while improvement unless the mind and body are given proper attention. Although a good shooter needs advanced equipment, but conversely, good equipment does not alone always make a good shooter. Pistol shooters need years of experience in the sport before they may hope to attain elite of achievement in competition.

AIR PISTOL TARGET SHOOTING

Target shooting is an indoor and outdoor sport in which contestant fire small arms at stationary targets and training target, as distinguished from catapulted targets used in trapshooting. The standard target is a square thick paper with concentric black and white rings around a black circular centre known as the bull's-eye. The object in target-shooting contests is to place a series of shots inside the bull's-eye. Pistol matches are contested with various classes and calibers of firearms.

In shooting, air pistol is a one of the newer forms and provides the beginner with a good introduction to the shooting sport. Air pistol shooters use static targets and firing position. Apart from other factors responsible for the performance, sight picture and aiming also has great impact to air pistol shooter. Air pistol is the best option for learning the basic skills of shooting accurately because, the lack of recoil means you get to see exactly what effect your trigger release has on sight alignment. Secondly the lack of noise builds confidence in novice shooters who are not yet accustomed to real guns. In air pistol shooting (caliber .177) competitors stand at a firing line 10 meters from the target. The task is to hold the pistol as steadily as possible, aiming at the target, while smoothly squeezing a trigger, which takes 500g of pressure to release. This is a very difficult task, and to repeat it perfectly for 60 shots demands the most rigid mental discipline. A world class shooter makes around 590/600 (men) or 390/400 (women), which means only ten shots fail to hit the bull's eye.

Air pistol shooting joined the Olympic program in 1988. Competitions use .177 caliber pistols to fire lead pellets at targets 10 meters away. The bull eye has a

AIR PISTOL TARGET SHOOTING

11.5mm (.45 inch) 10-rings. Therefore it is stated that air pistol shooting is designed to test "pure marksmanship". Air pistol matches consist of 60 shots for men and 40 shots for women and junior. On the air pistol target, scoring rings 7 through 10 are black with the 10 ring a tiny 12 mm.

One of the best developments in 10-meter competition came in 1986 with the advent of "finals". This is currently used in all major matches worldwide. Introduction of the finals in the air pistol shooting has certainly added a dramatic and interesting new element for the spectator. Results and ranking order are instantly and comprehensively displayed in numbers. There are obvious favorites and infavorites. The continuous fluctuation in the ranking during the 10 shots of the finals makes excitement up to the last shot.

The method is as follow. After the 60 shot match is completed, the top 8 competitors are placed in the order they finished the 60 shot match on the line-first place on position #1, second on #2, etc. They then begin a 10 shot finals shoot-off. In this final, the competitors have a 75 second time limit to fire each shot. After the last competitor has fired shot number 1, the targets are scored, and the score is read out. The competitors then shoot shot number 2, after which the scoring is again done, and so on through all 10 shots. The scoring of each shot is given a numerical value to the tenth of a point. The lowest possible shot for score would be a 1.0 with the pellet just touching the outside of the lowest value scoring ring. The highest value shot would be a 10.9, or a perfect center shot. This 10.9 maximum value rule has been in place since 1989 when the 11.0 value

AIR PISTOL TARGET SHOOTING

was dropped by .1 of a point. The maximum score now possible is 709.0 with the 10 shot finals included. That would be sixty consecutive tens, followed by ten consecutive 10.9 shots.

Now a days, success has become the ultimate aim of players, sports personnel and the society in general. Shooting is a very fast growing sports and one in which India's shooters are achieving considerable success at international level. It is shooting only in which India could secure silver medal in 2004 Olympics. This is the only silver medal India won in any individual event (not only shooting) for the last 104 years. Media has become more focused on spectator sports and less interested in sports like shooting. The air pistol shooting was not a spectator sport; therefore there was little scope for a competitive shooter to turn professional. With the introduction of the electronic target systems the seen is changed. Shooting also has started to become spectacular.

The elite shooter should have complete shooting technique that is straightforward and uncomplicated; all movements and action should be executed unsurprisingly and naturally, the body and the hand holding pistol moving together as one familiar unit. The whole shooter, from head to feet, will be self-possessed and balanced with no unnecessary tension in any area; emotionally and physically relaxed, but alert. The head should neither hinder nor compromise the development of an anatomically efficient shot. The structure of the face and the lower jaw should be used only to position the controlling aiming eye consistently behind the sight picture at a fixed height. Meanwhile the brain will examine and confirm, by the feel of the body actions that the series will be proficiently accomplished. All body actions, movements and positions will take benefit of any unavoidable loads imposed by the natural laws of physics to minimize the expenditure of energy. There should be no disagreement between the proficient use of mind and body and the demands essential to make use of the competence of the equipment.

A variety of mental disciplines must offer the control required to uphold self-assurance, sustained repetition of performance, positive thinking, avoidance of over-confidence, exclusion of negativity and dejection. For the above said factors, mastery of the bodily expertise alone is not adequate to meet the elements of technique essential to uphold scores high enough. Psychological discipline, producing ability for strong attentiveness will provide for this necessary demanding control. The shooter's ability of coordination skill, his natural talent to endure training, his bodily condition, his mental discipline and control and the appropriateness and his equipment will give release of one correct shot on the target.

THE HISTORY OF SHOOTING SPORT

People have always been fascinated by weaponry. At one time a civilian, who had the prestige to carry arms, was considered to be an important or special person in the society. Many times arms were banned due to its royal perspective. In the ancient times, these weapons were daggers and close quarter spears, then bows, and slings. The primary function of these weapons was for hunting and occasionally for self-defense against rival tribes and animals. The skill of gunfire had a various character extended before it became a sport. Shooting dates back to man's most primitive origins as spear-throwing fight and improved hunting expertise. Every modern sport has some history before becoming a competitive sport.

The hypotheses of the beginning or origin of the shooting is not completely realistic, and it is not properly explored so far. We may agree to that the individuality of a discoverer will never be acknowledged for certain. But what we can be sure of, is that when gunpowder appeared it revolutionized and modernized the art of conflict and warfare.

The conventional hunting was subjugated by the crossbow before the beginning of gunpowder to the western hemisphere. The gunpowder had slight effect on the long established traditions of hunting and the conventional hunting arms like the longbow and crossbow were hard for more efficient and perfect hunting than fire arms.

A few historians articulate that the Persians or the Greeks discovered the gunpowder, while others state that a Franciscan monk named Berthold Schwarz who was born in Germany in 14th century invented it. Ammunition is an inseparable part of the shooting itself and it is chiefly described in the caliber of the weapon and it is on purpose to fitting.

Though firearm machinery has advanced and has become sophisticated extremely over the centuries, the key principles remain the same: a metal pipe closed at one end with a small opening made or left in it. The

AIR PISTOL TARGET SHOOTING

gunpowder and the projectile were fed into the open end of the pipe and rammed to the far end. The gunpowder was then burst into flames through the little opening and projectile-usually a stone or other metal ball was shot from the pipe. The discovery of the wheel-lock made the pistol a practicable proposition. The wheel-lock is a metal disc combined with a coil spring. Some of the early wheel-lock pistols of the late sixteenth and seventeenth centuries were not simply good-looking weapons, chased and gilded and engraved, but accurate and hard hitting. These appear to have been more popular than rifled muskets, because being shorter in the barrel they were not so difficult to load.

Screw-barreled pistol of which the rifled barrel could be unscrewed from the butt so that the ball and charge could be loaded into tne breech, were not uncommon. Wheel-locks were expensive and complicated but the flint-lock pistol was a cheap and common weapon, carried by every cavalry trooper.

For the duration of the eighteenth century the pistol progressively put back the rapier/ sword as the duelist's favorite weapon, especially in England, Ireland and America where the flag of swordsmanship was generally low. The customary technique of firing was with the pistol almost at arm's length, the elbow almost straight. Some fired in an awkward, cramped position, the arm bent and the elbow down so as to give some protection to the body.

Contest were occasionally fought on horse back, the revelries firing as they galloped past one another their pistols charged eithe. with ball or with swan-short. In 1665 in France Madame de la Pre-Abbe and Mademoislle de la Motte fought such a duel. Dueling

8

AIR PISTOL TARGET SHOOTING

achieved its full ridiculousness in the early twentieth century when dueling pistols were intentionally made to be almost inoffensive. The barrels were so deficiently bored and the trigger-pull was so rigid. There were pistols made to be similar to daggers or riding whips. These pistols were so tiny and had less usefulness.

For the period of three centuries all effectual pistols were single or double barreled, single or two shot weapons. The automatic pistol emerged in the late nineteenth century. There are innumerable manufacturers and patterns, but all based on the same principle. When the wheel-lock is released by squeezing the trigger, the pressure of the spring causes the metal disc to spin backwards, scraping against a flint as it does. This causes a shower of sparks that ignites the fine gunpowder in the pan. This technique is still widely used for modern cigarette lighters. The flint was secured in the jaws of a kind of hammer. This cock/hammer as it is called was fixed to the side of the weapon and could be drawn backwards against the tension of the spring and locked into position. When the trigger was pressed the flint struck a metal plate close to the flash hole. The resulting sparks ignited the gunpowder in the flash hole.

Hitting/percussion explosion/ignition was the foremost footstep in the advancement of firearms. A Scottish priest, Alexander Forsyth invented the percussion primer. Around 1820, a highly explosive chemical composite was developed that could be lodged in a minute cap. The difficulty of using an exposed flame for ignition became a thing of the past.

The manufacture of cartridge is the next most important step in the history of firearms. The

AIR PISTOL TARGET SHOOTING

components of the cartridge were gun powder, percussion cap and brass case and they were assembled in one unit. Cartridge had to be placed in the chamber of the barrel through the back of the fire arm. This meant that the rear of the barrel had to be open to load the weapon. The bolt-action chamber was used to close the barrel to prevent it from splitting or springing open when the charge exploded. The pin fire system or rim fire cartridge was the other form of cartridge. In rim fire cartridge ignition is molded into the rim of the cartridge-case it self. This is ignited by a blow from the hammer against a protruding pin at the rear of the cartridge case. This ammunition is still used widely in small caliber weapons. The invention of nitro-powder was also a great step in the development of weapons. This led to the development of semi-automatic weapons.

Community shooting festivals have been held in some northern European cities, since the sixteenth century. The modern world wide interest in target shooting, however, dates really from the second half of the nineteenth century. This was result of technical advances in firearms. Shooting disciplines differ as to the distance, form of the target, the exact nature of the firearm and ammunition used, the position of the firer, and timing and number of the shots fired.

At that time shooting contest usually was one-shot competition fired at decorated wooden targets. These contests were customarily organized on festival/celebration and awards were generally of gold. In 1710, target shooting made its way to the United States and the events were called "turkey shoots", at first with food items being the prizes. In the 1790s, the U.S. developed

AIR PISTOL TARGET SHOOTING

match rifles with long barrel and double-set trigger features. By 1825, formal match shooting began and trapshooting contests followed five years later. Countries began forming their own national federations around the same time and eight nations formed the International Shooting Union or UIT (Union International De Tir). It was formed at Zurich in 1907 which, controlled international events. Shooting was an event at the 1896 Olympic Games in Athens and missed only the 1904 and 1928 Games. In the first Olympic Games only four shooting events were introduced and in next Games in Paris, the number of events was increased to seven. Clay-pigeon shooting (individual), running deer shooting, single shot (individual), army rifle (team), pistol any target 50m., pistol or revolver (team) and automatic pistol or revolver (individual) were these events. Shooting was dropped in 1928 Games because of a controversy in the IOC about the definition of an "amateur" in the shooting. In the next Games, this matter was settled. The shooting again figured in 1936 Olympics and the I.O.C. decided that a shooter would be allowed to take part if he had not received a money prize for shooting since August 1, 1934.

Development of the Air Pistol

By means of our attraction for weaponry we can mechanically use hobby shooting, target shooting or competition shooting as a course of accomplishing self-mastery. Air weapons sometimes called garden/hobby weapons, are in unpretentious class of weapon and chiefly practical for schooling new learners. Air weapons are trouble-free to preserve and are within the reach of most of the people as they are cheap. Air weapons do not

AIR PISTOL TARGET SHOOTING

require license.

Formerly the coil/spring power-driven pistols were of the moving piston kind. In these types of air arms, a compressed spring drives a piston in a cylinder compressing the air volume and driving a pellet through the barrel. These kinds of air arms were not accurate as the movement of the spring results in recoil, which tends to throw the pistol off the aiming area.

The manufacturer of the modern air pistol Feinwerkbau produced the moving piston air pistol, Model 65 and Model 80. These pistols had modifiable/ changeable sight and very high accuracy. With the development of model 65 and 80 some modifications have taken place in accuracy and precision. Feinwerkbau Model 90 followed these well-liked models with an electronic trigger, which has consistent trigger weight at the time of firing. The formal type of competition was developed to take advantage of their incredible accuracy and precision. The trigger worked off a 15-volt battery. The new generation of Pneumatic and Carbon dioxide propelled air pistols were inspired by the improved standard of shooting. The forerunner of the modern pistols Feinwerkbau produced the first CO2 Match Pistol, Feinwerkbau Model 2. It had a cylinder below the barrel, which could be filled from a fire-extinguisher type cylinder and fitted to the pistol. This permitted the shooter to fire about 200 shots with no attempt of cocking and recoil. The additional benefit was the low center of gravity since the bulk of the pistol was below the shooter's hand. Walther simultaneously launched their CP2 a heavier pistol with good large sights.

AIR PISTOL TARGET SHOOTING

To fulfill the requirements of the rapid fire shooters Walther and Feinwerkbau launched 5 shot repeating CO_2 powered pistols. These pistols could not acquire much good turn since the set of laws did not permit their use in contests and were expensive training aids.

New-fangled companies like Air Match and Pardini Fiochhi produced fine compressed air pistols and the Germans almost immediately had competition from the Italian firearm industry. Problems of inconsistency and unreliability overwhelmed these pistols and they were not very well liked. Therefore Feinwerkbau presented their Model 100 and 102 sequence of pneumatic pistol with their well-known and legendary reliability.

Walther immediately reacted with a like model the LP1. The CO_2 pistols had a disadvantage of unreliable and unstable pressure at different levels of CO_2 gas. The subsequently new production of pistols the Feinwerkbau Model 10 and the Walther CP2 Match had a staging chamber built in to compensate for varying cylinder pressures. This improvement had taken one step higher with the Feinwerkbau Model 25 and the Walther renovation to a vertically mounted cylinder to avoid liquid CO_2 leaking into the chamber during firing.

Though CO_2 pistols had comparatively small amount recoil they did have a small kick as the pellet was released from the barrel. An Austrian company, Steyr launched a model with a compensator. This attachment to the muzzle of the pistol vented the residual CO_2 upwards to counter-act the effects to the jump. These compensated Air Pistols were seen on all the ranges. Walther and Feinwerkbau offered their models CPM 1 and the Model C20 and C25 correspondingly, with

AIR PISTOL TARGET SHOOTING

compensators. One elite shooter had blamed his CO2 pistol for one bad shot and this kicked off the hunt for a new propellant.

Morini a Swiss company brings in a pistol powered by compressed air. The cylinder is charged with air at a pressure of 3000 psi. This required a valve that worked across a wide range of pressures and a vigorous device. Nowadays, Morini and Hammerli, the renowned firearm manufacturers, offer their models of compressed air pistols. The Morini is an aluminium cylindered electronically fired air pistol while the Hammerli is a Hi-tech pistol with a cylinder of aluminium wrapped in Carbon Fiber. The Morini works on compressed air only while the Hammerli can be charged with CO2 or Air. The compressed air is usually provided through a diving bottle and is relatively easy to use. All these pistols offer an accurate, high precision piece of equipment, which will give years and years of trouble free service. They are cheap to shoot and will grind your skills to world beating standards. Steyr and Feinwerkbau have introduced their compressed air powered pistols and their designers are working hard on the next Models. The major forerunners of the modern pistols are Feinwerkbau, Steyr, Morini, Walther and Hammerli.

By the advent of finals and the electronic scoring monitors used at world-class competitions, air pistol shooting has become something of a spectator sport. Some major changes have taken place in just the last two decades. In 1980, the UIT changed the men's competition from a 40 to a 60 shot format. Women's competition stayed at 40 shots and has remained there since. Also in 1980 the firing of sighter shots was

AIR PISTOL TARGET SHOOTING

changed, allowing unlimited shots- but all had to be taken before the first record shot. Now, according to ISSF rules, a ten-minute preparation period is given before the match starts. The duration of time a competitor has during a match has been shortened from two hours, to just one hour and forty-five minutes including sighter shots for men and for women the time is one hour and fifteen minutes for the 40 shot match including sighters.

SAFETY-REQUIREMENTS

Safety rhyme:

> If a sport man your would be,
>
> listen carefully to me,
>
> Never, never, let your gun
>
> pointed be at anyone.
>
> That is may unloaded be
>
> matters not the least to me.
>
> — Maurice Turner

Safety is absolutely essential for proper management of the firearms. Actually the original aim of firearms is to take life/destroy and they will fulfill the purpose whether fired deliberately or accidentally. The degree of safety necessary in the handling of a pistol needs to be far greater than with a rifle, because a minor movement of the hand, which is holding it, can cause the muzzle to sweep a large arc, due to the compact nature of the weapon.

In fact, shooting sports is remarkably free from accident and injuries. Most accidents are due to

AIR PISTOL TARGET SHOOTING

carelessness or failure to observe the elementary safety rules. There are two of the most important aspects of safety in the shooting sport - range safety and proper handling of firearms. All the participants must be familiar with the appropriate rules and regulations of shooting sport to ensure safe shooting. Few safety guidelines are as follow:

- Handle every pistol as if it were loaded at all times.

- Store weapons out of the reach of children; never aim a pistol at anyone, even if you are sure it is not loaded.

- Do not leave your firearm unattended and transport your weapons dismantled and in a lockable carrying case if possible.

- On a shooting range, always follow the instructions of the session leader/range officer.

- Pistol, whether at the firing point or not, must always be unloaded, unless otherwise instructed by the Range Officer.

- Get permission from the owner before pick up a weapon that does not belong to you and treat it as it is loaded.

- Pistols kept at home should be stored in a safe, and do not assume that your weapon is safe.

- Pistol must never be loaded except when on the firing point and the front of the firing point must be clear.

AIR PISTOL TARGET SHOOTING

- Keep the actions open except when aiming at the intended target.

- No horseplay on the range.

- Every person is responsible for safety and every one may call a "Cease Fire" upon observing an unsafe act.

- Always prove the pistol when handling it.

- Keep pistol and ammunition separate as far as possible and keep firearms and ammunition safe and know your ammunition.

- Do not change targets until all the pistols on the firing point are unloaded.

- When dry firing a pistol, always point it at something safe.

- Discipline is essential and required on the range if accidents are to be prevented.

- Never point any firearm at anyone unless you intend to shoot him. This also applies even when the pistol has been checked and is proved to be unloaded.

- Never load pistol unless, and until, you intend to shoot, and even then not until given permission to load by the Range Officer. Unload your pistol as soon as you have finished using it and point your pistol out of harm's way while you are doing this.

AIR PISTOL TARGET SHOOTING

- Once a firearm is loaded always be conscious of this fact and always keep the gun/pistol pointed towards the target end of the range.

EQUIPMENTS AND ACCESSORIES

In recent years many manufacturers have put more endeavors into bringing new kinds of accessories than into developing their collection of armaments. Although compared to some other games, pistol-shooting equipment turn out to be quite technical, though the sport itself is not. It is a sport of the mind and body just like any other. There are so many shooters in the expedition for enhancement search for the invalid method of additional apparatus. The only way to perk up scores is all the way through schooling of mind and body and no quantity of sophisticated equipments, will make a worth-while enhancement unless the mind and body are given appropriate consideration.

Although a fine shooter requires excellent equipment, it does not mean that a good quality apparatus alone can create an excellent shooter. Apart from the pistol there are some necessary items and some to make shooting successful. The shooter should have a most up-to-date knowledge of ISSF Rules and Regulations and he should then familiarize himself with the rules concerning the weapons. Because each make and model can vary in respect of size, weight, balance, sight length and composition, barrel length, distance from back strap to trigger, size and position of the trigger, size and rake of grip, etc. A manufacturer cannot produce a grip that will suit every hand that will hold it.

AIR PISTOL TARGET SHOOTING

Air pistol shooting is a sport that does require equipment other than a pistol. Even a shooter who is only beginning to shoot should have basic accessories available. In target pistol shooting you must acquire some special equipment like any other specialized sport. It would be worthwhile buying such items as earmuffs, for example for safeguarding your ears. Safety is important at all times and in addition to protection, earmuffs enable you to concentrate. The essential accessories are anything to do with maintaining and carrying your pistol and include carrying cases, eye blinders, earmuffs, dairy etc. Unlike most other sport, there is no special clothing for pistol shooting and you can wear what you feel most comfortable in.

Pistol

Air pistol shooting discipline has limitations upon the pistol that can be used in this event, so that if a pistol does not meet the requirements it cannot be used. In these days, the manufacturers of the competition pistols make pistols to the limits of the competition requirements. As there are many secondhand pistols available in the market for resale that may be outside the permitted dimensions. So it will be better to buy a new pistol for perfect working order.

It is suggested that in target pistol shooting you must acquire good quality pistol. The shooters must have their own pistol for better performance. The developing beginner to the sport of target pistol shooting should consider the following factors critical in the purchase of a target pistol. These are reliability and accuracy, sights, trigger action, weight and balance, grip and cost

AIR PISTOL TARGET SHOOTING

of pistol. There are some manufactures of air pistol that have a status, trustworthiness and reliability. Some backdrop information is therefore presented in the hope that it may assist the novice to make those plans somewhat easier to put together. In choosing pistol the key consideration is the monetary question, but try not to let this limit your choice too rigidly. It is well worth expenditure a little more in order to make long-lasting asset and good pistols have good resale value. The shooter should not buy pistol strictly upon price alone and stick with the major brands in choosing his pistol. The shooter should opt for a pistol that is right for his purpose and it should fit into his hand comfortably. There are some manufacturers of air pistol, have a reputation and reliability like Feinwerkbau, Styer, Moini and Wolther. The P40 Feinwerkbau and LP20 Styer is the top-of-the-line air pistol these days.

Trigger

The option of the trigger depends upon the shooter. It can have short area of travel or a long one and it can be wide or narrow. It is a significant thing to consider that the trigger must require a consistent amount of pressure in order to release a shot or to fire the pistol. The semi-automatic pistols are fitted with special dry firing mechanisms. A trigger should be crispy and predictable.

Sights

The sight radius, the distance between the front and rear sight and quality micrometer sights with positive click stops are important considerations for sights selection. Sights must be open and it should be adjustable horizontally and vertically.

Grip

Grip is an essential part to fit the pistol to the shooter's hand. Wooden grips are preferable to plastic/synthetic ones. The grip should allow the shooter to take a correct hold of pistol in relation to natural sight alignment, independent movement of the trigger finger and comfort. Grip can be modified/customized to the desire of each individual shooter by the shooter or gunsmith.

Corrective lenses and shooting glasses

Your vision, just like the strength and endurance in your arms and legs, is an important part of your overall performance. There are a few accessory items used by all shooters but the first and most important is vision and hearing protection. The demands on your visual system during sporting activities are rigorous. To shoot your best, you must be able to sight your target, and this takes a variety of vision skills. If your natural vision inhibits your performance, ask your doctor about corrective lenses.

Today's eye care practitioners utilize a wide variety of lens materials. One such development is the new impact-resistant lens now available for use in prescription glasses. These lenses are cosmetically excellent, reasonable in cost, lightweight, and will not shatter if broken. It is an individual decision, and you may want to try shooting with and without glasses to see which works best for you.

AIR PISTOL TARGET SHOOTING

Another option is contact lenses. Available in hard and soft lens materials, contacts offer many excellent advantages to the athlete. For best results, tell your doctor about the type of sports you play. That information will be helpful to the doctor in selecting the best lenses for you. If you wear contact lenses, take your cleaning and wetting solutions with you to all shooting events, and notify your coach that you are wearing contacts.

Getting a foreign object in the eye is the most common eye problem associated with shooting sports. Fortunately, these foreign objects are usually in the form of minor irritants such as dust, dirt, and sand. Glasses will help to protect your eyes form ammunition blowback and similar dangers. There are many styles to choose from - select one that fits securely and provides the best vision. The shooting glasses can enhance sight definition and reduce eye fatigue.

Hearing protection

It is considered must for the protection of ears/ hearing. There are two types of ear protectors -earplugs and earmuffs and the final choice depends upon the shooter's preference. However, it is important that whichever is chosen is suitable for the purpose. Hearing protection is always used on the pistol range. Good quality earplugs and/ or earmuffs will help to prevent hearing damage and improve concentration by reducing audio distractions. Even though the report of a small bore cartridge is not particularly loud, continual exposure to pistol firing, especially indoors, will cause a hearing loss. The good quality earmuff type is required to reduce noise sufficiently. The plug type ear defenders may be rubber /fitted plastic. The help shut out odd noises conversation and distraction, but must fit properly. Good plugs provide good protection but you should be able to hear the instructions from the range officer or scorekeeper.

Notebook / Shooting Dairy

Notebook is an important accessory for a shooter. All the top shooters keep shooting dairy. Shooter should have a pen and a scorebook that will enable them to store information to be used in future practice and matches. This also will help in analyzing the scores in addition to the technical and mechanical aspects of shooting. Details regarding sight setting, score and such other important details can be noted in the dairy. The shooting dairy can be a valuable aid in mental management and one should record problems and solutions. The notebook serves numerous purposes, which include: a. score recording; b. notes on training and match, c. notes on shooting positions and d. general range information. And it is important that the entries should be of positive aspects of performance, successes and strong points of the shooter.

Stop Watch

An electronic type or digital stopwatch should be easily readable figures. It helps to note the shooting time, and shot intervals between the series of shot. A stopwatch helps the shooter to find out how much time is left to complete the match. A wristwatch is a good substitute.

AIR PISTOL TARGET SHOOTING

Shooting Cap

Shooting cap is an optional accessory. Shooting cap will prevent the light falling on the shooting glasses directly.

Electronic Scoring Target

The Electronic Scoring target system comprises a simulated target with its own electronic scoring mechanism, a firing point monitor, a printer to record the shot value and a remote display for spectators. The face of a target is a white card without scoring rings. In the center is a hole, which is the size of the black portion of the selected target.

Miscellaneous equipments

A box or bag is desirable to carry the miscellaneous smaller items of equipment, which may be used to aid the shooter. In these days air pistol comes in a foam-lined hard-plastic case with cutouts for a second air cylinder, assorted wrenches, sight-adjustment screwdriver, a nipple for releasing air pressure out of the charging cylinder, a pressure gauge, and a DIN filling nipple. Wash-leather or towels for wet weather is useful. A cotton handkerchief or cloth is always good for wiping of sweat in hot weather. Each individual shooter can have his own kit list, which may well include additional items, which are not mentioned here.

DOMINANT EYE

For the reason of distance between the eyes, it is impossible to use both. We cannot control which eye

AIR PISTOL TARGET SHOOTING

will dominate. Eye dominance, like hand dominance, is something you are born with. Most people have a dominant eye - one that perceives the detail whilst the other adds the perspective. This is usually the same as their laterality so that right - handed people have a dominant right eye. The determining factor is whether your strong hand and your strong eye are on the same side. Every person is aware of hand dominance, but many people are unaware that they also have a dominant eye. The beginner must be tested for eye dominance and it helps to find out whether the individual fire left or right hand has to be used. The individual is termed as ipsi lateral if the dominant eye is on the same side as the dominant hand. If the dominant eye is on the opposite side from the dominant hand, the individual has contra lateral hand eye dominance. The biomechanical problems with contra lateral hand-eye dominance have an effect on the pistol shooting, even though the pistol is held at arm's length. If an arm is extended to hold the weight of a pistol, the shooter normally stands with his/her legs spread somewhat and with more weight shifted in the direction opposite the pistol. If the contra lateral eye is used, the body must be shifted, twisting slightly to allow that eye proper alignment on the sights. This seemingly insignificant shift would naturally move the center of gravity toward the pistol, causing the shooter to be slightly off balance. The resulting position requires more effort to maintain and is more fatiguing. The current research supports the emphasis on the use of the dominant eye and non-dominant hand for those individuals who indicate contra lateral hand-eye dominance.

AIR PISTOL TARGET SHOOTING

Miller Cone Test

The miller cone test is a legendary procedure for testing eye dominance. In this method the shooter cups his hands in front of his eyes leaving a small opening between his hands. A helper, standing 6-8 feet away holds up an object/article such as a ball. Then, the shooter should focus on the object through the cone with both eyes open. The coach then determines which eye is observing the object through the cone. This will be your dominant eye. Figure 4.1.(I)

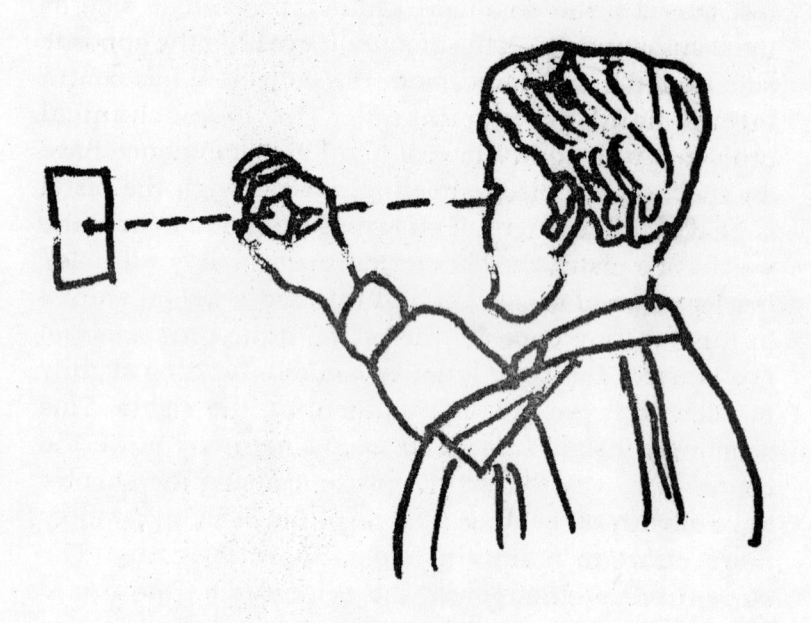

Fig. 1. Determining the Dominent/Master Eye

AIR PISTOL TARGET SHOOTING

Largely people are best recommended to shoot with both eyes open. Assuring your eye and hand dominance is on the same side you will generally find that shooting with both eyes open will give you the best advantage. With both eyes open your peripheral vision and depth perceptions are enhanced. If you are cross-dominant (i.e. right-handed person with dominant left eye or vice-versa) then there may be very good reason to close one eye as you shoot.

⟨2⟩

Essentials of Good Shooting Skills

STANCE-POSITION

Except in some specialized pistol shooting outside the realms of normal target shooting it is always necessary to stand unsupported, hold the pistol at arm's length also unsupported, aim and fire. The object of the stance is to bring the shooter into position, so that when he takes aim his pistol aligns with the target without conscious effort.

The accuracy of shooting and the degree of immobility of the pistol need serious attention to the stance. It is insufficient merely to assume a convenient and stable stance but you must be able to aim at your target in a natural and consistent manner. Before you can fire a shot you must adopt the correct stance so that the pistol can be fired accurately with a consistent close grouping of shots.

Stance is a personal matter for each shooter because of the varying heights, body shapes and muscular developments of different shooters. Therefore, there is no single definition and hard rule of correct stance. On the other hand the stance should be suitable to your kinathropometric status and physical characteristics of body. The stance of all shooters can't be defined because every shooter possesses certain individualities and characteristics. Therefore, the shooter may adopt his/her own stance/natural stance, suitable for his/her body.

Each shooter has a different comfortable position, which will be his/her natural stance. It cannot be assumed that each shooter will adopt exactly the same stance every time. The shooter must take up his natural stance each time he/she takes up his/her firing position. Standing ready to fire on a fixed-point, the shooter will adopt an approximate position, which generally suits him/her. The main objective of the natural stance is to provide a stable shooting platform. The shooter must support the extended arm holding a pistol and maintain his body in a stable position. The stance must provide the maximum immobility and the minimum strain to the muscles/body of the shooter.

In the early stage of training any type of incorrect stance must be corrected. When assuming the firing stance, there must not be strain in the knee joints and leg muscles, which will lead to a loss of stability. The human body has a natural position for every requirement and the stance must be comfortable.

The rules for normal pistol shooting stipulate that the shooter must be unaided and hold the pistol in one hand at arms length without artificial aids. The body must therefore be capable of adopting a sufficiently

AIR PISTOL TARGET SHOOTING

stable position to hold the pistol to produce within the required parameter a top score. The body must acquire the most stable position it can if the shooter is going to function efficiently. The considerations involved are the environment need to exercise as precise a control as possible over the pistol, and the fitness of the shooter. You should avoid unnecessary muscular effort or strain. Only certain amount of muscular effort is required in order to stand in the aim position. Certain muscles are used to keep the body erect to hold the arm outstretched and to hold the pistol. These muscles must be given rest to avoid the undue weakness. The periodical relaxation allows a muscle to recover from any previous exertion. This will help to reduce the excessive muscular tension, which has an adverse effect upon the nature of movement of the shooting arm.

Kinesthetic sense or proprioceptiveness is the sense, which provides the individual with an awareness of the position of his/her body or parts of body with respect to space. The receptors are stimulated by the stress placed on them usually by movement itself and when this information is processed, the individual is able in varying degrees of efficiency to determine the position of his/her body in space and to control. As kinesthetic sense gives an individual the "feel" or the "touch", or an awareness of his body in space, it is essential to all coordinated movements of stance and position. Such awareness appears to be an important factor in learning the appropriate stance. The "self-knowledge" or "awareness of body" also helps in the learning process of various fundamentals of neuromuscular movements and skills in shooting.

AIR PISTOL TARGET SHOOTING

The first aspect in stance to be considered is the contact between the body and the ground, assuming that the body is right. The stability of the firing arm and weapons depends to an extent upon the correct placement of the feet, which determines the support area for the shooter's body. The placement of the feet creates a comparatively large support area and reduces the muscular strain in the legs. Too close placement of legs decreases the support area and will result in a loss of stability. In comfortable stance, the muscles of both legs will be carrying the same load during extended arm holding a weapon.

The feet should be placed approximately shoulder width apart with the balance of the body slightly forward on the toes to reduce tension in the leg muscles. The legs must be straight, with as many muscles as possible relaxed and the knees should be straight but not taut. The trunk must be straight, in the natural line of body. The neck must also be relaxed. The head should be erect so as to ensure the most effective use of the eyes and if the non-shooting eye is closed the facial muscles are not to be tightened. The shoulders must be completely relaxed so that the only muscles being used are those necessary to hold the arm out. Directly required muscles are to be used for aiming the pistol and they should therefore be relaxed as much as possible. The excessive muscular tension is fault in which the unnecessary tension in the muscles used for shooting.

To avoid the disturbance to the natural balance of the body, the natural position is suggested. If the natural position is adopted there is great possibility of stability. The feet should be placed apart according to shoulders

AIR PISTOL TARGET SHOOTING

and the body weight evenly distributed over the sole of your feet. Therefore the stance must be natural, position and your body must be balanced and firm and yet without strain. This should allow your hand holding the pistol to point naturally towards the target. Basically the correct stance is the best position that the body can adopt to hold the pistol at arm's length with the minimum of muscular effort. The correctness of the assumed position must be checked before each shot. In the normal position the average shooter faces about 40° to 50° away from the target.

In the correct shooting position the body-pistol system is placed in the correct relationship to the target and for this there is no necessity to move the arm. The precise position of the feet in relation to the line of fire will vary from person to parson but their position in relation to the body will alter very little. We have to rely on two legs and therefore have to position the feet along two sides of a triangle to get a comfortable position.

The best position is along the sides of an equilateral triangle, which lie within the width of the shooters shoulders. The heels should be about twelve inches apart at an angle of 60°. Individual modifications to this will depend on the shooters physique. The center of gravity of the body will be above the center of triangle and there will be no necessity for the shooter to lean forward or backward to maintain his position. The purpose of the erect posture is to hold the head in such a position that the eyes can be used most effectively looking straight ahead and parallel to the ground. The head can then be turned in any direction without strain. To see the target directly in line with the arm and through the sights the head must be held straight and tilting the head to the right or left may interrupt sights alignment stability of pistol.

There should be no apparent strain in holding the pistol and standing in correct position. The body should be relaxed and the pelvis should hold the weight of the trunk. If the body is too tense 'sway' (movement) will develop. Sway will also occur if the feet are too close or too far apart. The non-shooting arm should be used as a counter weight to balance the body-against the weight of the other outstretched arm, but it must be completely relaxed. The free hand may be inserted into the side pocket in a relaxed manner, or you may hook the thumb of the free handover the waist belt. The free arm must not be in loose hanging position, because slightest movement of this arm may be transferred to the body. The shooter must be consistent in his/her footwear because, the link between the body and the ground is through footwear. Shoes should have flexible uppers and the sole should be flat to provide full contact between the feet and the ground.

GRIP

The main object of a good grip is to give the shooter the utmost degree of possession over maintaining a natural sight alignment. The grip helps and supports to produce a good shot. Maintaining the sight alignment should be easy during aiming and shooting. The holding of the grip should be firm enough while firing a shot. Any type of altering or slipping of the grip will upset the natural sight alignment. There must be no altering in the stiffness/tightness of the grip while firing a shot

AIR PISTOL TARGET SHOOTING

because it will unfavorably effect sight alignment. The pressure of the holding must remain steady and the strengthening or loosening of the hold will cause loss of control of the grip.

Prior to making the grasp/grip the shooter must be acquainted with the method of gripping. The non-shooting hand (left for right handed and right for left handed) is used to pick the pistol. The key technique is to grasp or hold the pistol (in case of right hand) using an overhand grip. Then open the right hand, making a "V" between the thumb and forefinger. Then the middle of "V" is positioned against the back of the pistol grip, as high up as possible, keeping the fingers extended. The lower three fingers should come to relax and rest closely touching each other. Then the second and third fingers are curled round the front of the grip. Force will be exerted by the muscles of the hand holding the pistol grip back against the ball of the thumb. The little finger can curl unaffectedly and be used if suitable to facilitate the other two fingers. The little finger must not affect/apply much pressure on the front strap because it may cause the muzzle to depress/lower slightly. This will adversely effect sight alignment. No force should be applied with the thumb but it should be seated on the thumb rest at the crest/top of the grip freely. The palm of the hand should make as much contact as possible with the grip, in order to achieve greater control over the pistol. Trigger pressure is an independent/autonomous act and the trigger finger should apply optimistic pressure on the trigger. The grip must be comfortable to delay tremble/shiver and overtiredness. Overtiredness affects the control of the pistol and trigger pressure.

AIR PISTOL TARGET SHOOTING

The grip should be taken as high up on the stock as possible. The higher the hand on the grip the smaller will be the movement. The most important element in the grip is consistency/uniformity. Change in group will be mostly due to slight changes in grip on the pistol. The grip must be made so that it can be picked up only in exactly the same way each and every time it is used.

The fitting of the grip must be comfortable/at ease and one must never force the hand into the grip as this will cause tension. The best for a well-fitting grip is the consistency of position of the group. It is almost certain that any change to the grip will also involve a shift in the position of the group. The grip should be solid/firm enough to make the pistol an extension of the arm. At the same time the grip must not be so firm that tremble/shiver is induced. Squeezing a rubber ball or using a spring-exerciser will help to develop good grip. Having acquired a standard grip, seek perfection and consistency through practice.

THE AIM

In pistol shooting aiming is an arguable feature and there are numerous dissimilar thoughts of specialists concerning the subject. Aiming is an act in which the shooter spaces the rear sight, front sight and aiming point in a single line in order to bring into line the pistol with the center of the target. The basic purpose of the aim is to arrange in a line the sights so that shot fired strike the core/center of the target.

The correct sight placement takes place, when the front sight is centered in the rear-sight notch and the tip of the front sight is positioned at the same level as the upper edges of the rear-sight notch. A sequence of shots is called a group and the axis of the group should be the center of the target. There are four key rudiments concerned in the aim; the target, the front or foresight, the rear or back sight, and the eye. Air pistols have modifiable rear sights and can be adjusted both vertically and laterally. The pistol will be aligned so that the point of aim, the tip of the foresight, the shoulders of the back sight, and the eye are in the same horizontal plane. The vertical plane will pass through the vertical axis of the target, the center of the tip of the foresight, the center of the notch in the rear sight and the eye. When these two planes cross, the pistol will be correctly aligned and if fired at that time, a shot will fall within the shooter's group.

The correct sight relationship is that the foresight will appear within the notch of the back sight with its top level with the shoulders of the back sight. There must be an equal amount of light through the notch of the back sight on either side of the foresight. The width of the foresight must not be too narrow or too wide. If the foresight is too narrow it will be harder to control the pistol and if it is too wide, it will be difficult to place on the required point of aim. Whatever widths are adopted the shooter must avoid eyestrain caused by trying to focus on too narrow a foresight. The width of the back sight notch should be about twice that of the foresight and its depth the same as the apparent with of the foresight.

Sight Picture

Sight picture is one more significant constituent of

aiming. The sight picture i.e. what the eye sees when looking through the sights at the target and focusing on the foresight. The correct sight relationship has to be seen against the target so that the eye can see the pattern that will be repeated time after time. Because it is reproduced frequently the brain will recognize correct sight picture. The point of aim is generally below the aiming mark into the white and the amount of white will depend on the individual shooter. The eye will see a strip of white between the aiming marks. If the sight relationship is correct any movement will be within the grouping capacity of the shooter and any shots outside that area will not be a sighting error.

Though the region of aim is well underneath the aiming mark, the group can be sited in the center of the target by adjusting the sights. Sight alteration should be a part of training program so that the shooters become skilled at how to amend their sights. Sight alternations should be made on the results of produced group of a bare minimum three shots. To decrease faults due to sight misplacement it is significant to preserve the correct sight correlation. If the shooter finds it hard to sustain the correct sight relationship it could be due to an erroneous stance or an incorrectly aligned grip. As the expertise of the shooter develops, the area of movement will lessen, the group will become smaller and the score will become higher.

Aiming Area: We cannot halt all movement of the pistol totally; therefore it is best to exert yourself on aiming area technique. It means to hold the pistol within the smallest possible arc of movement, with the sight perfectly aligned. This aiming area can be somewhere under the black of the target but not too close to it. A white gap under the black will make it easier to look at the sights.

Relationship of Sights

The pistol shooter is required to be conscious of the relationship of the rear sight and the foresight. The severely consciousness of this relationship will reduce the aiming errors known as angular shift errors.

Mostly the front sight is situated in different positions in the rear notch and this leads to a scattering of shots on the target. The sight alignment is the most critical of the angular shift and parallel shift error.

Sighting errors

The parallel and angular errors are two main sources of sighting errors. The parallel error is the deviating the hold of the aligned sights from the center of the aiming area. The angular error is the misalignment of the front sight in the rear sight notch. The parallel error is basically a holding error and is less hazardous than the angular error.

Figure 3.1. (II): Parallel Shift Error

AIR PISTOL TARGET SHOOTING

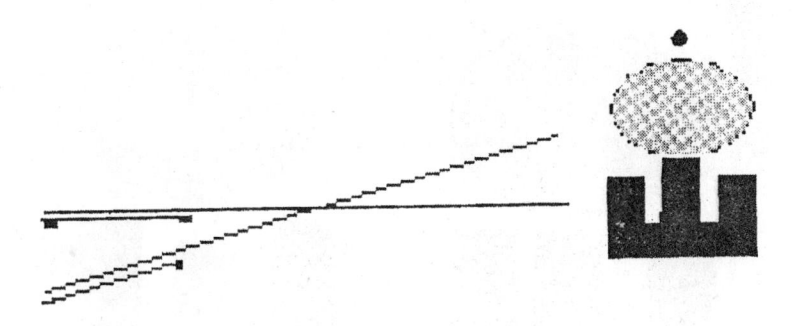

Figure 3.2. (II): Angular Shift Error

The correctness of a shot depends chiefly upon the shooter's ability to persistently uphold correct sight alignment. If the hold (arc of movement) is deviating in near parallel error from the center of the aiming area, it is established that these deflections will not lessen the score to the degree of angular shift error. If the sight alignment is good and hold is slightly high or low it will not affect the score as much as sight alignment to right or left.

It is difficult to maintain two sights in exact alignment while pressing the trigger without upsetting sight alignment. This needs comprehensive understanding and practice of correct sight alignment. The trouble comes in the complexity in maintaining a minimum arc of movement without disturbing sight alignment. Secondly the human eye cannot focus on a close-up object and a distant article simultaneously. When the dominating eye is focused on the target the comparatively little movement of the arm appears magnified. However, when the eye is correctly focused

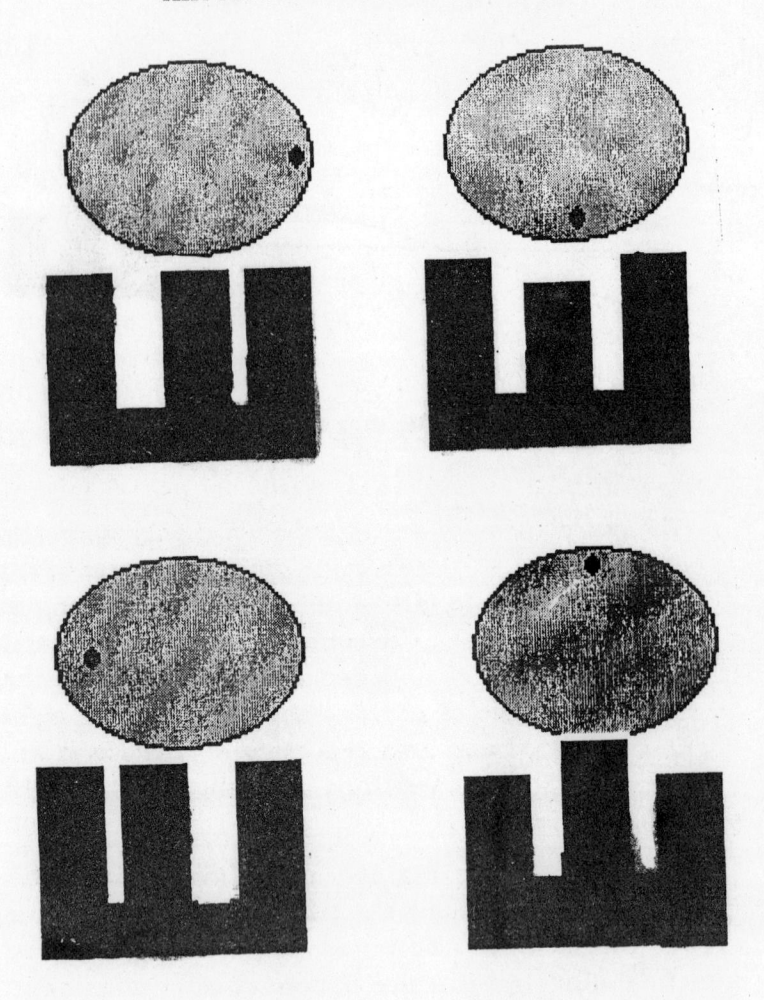

Figure 3.3 (II): Angular Shift Error

on the front sight this movement appears to have been reduced. For control alignment the focus should be limited to front sight only.

It is essential to uphold the front sight point of focus

AIR PISTOL TARGET SHOOTING

for the whole time of aiming of the pistol. The shooter must concentrate on maintaining the correct relationship between front and rear sight, and the point of the focus must be on the front sight during the short period required to deliver the shot. If the sights are incorrectly aligned, the net result is an inaccurate shot. Sight alignment must stay highest in the shooter's mind throughout the firing of the shot. In the preliminary stage of holding, the shooter has to line up the sight in a perfect manner. As the shooter is concentrating on delivering the shot, he frequently loses correct sight alignment, which he accomplished in the preliminary stage of his hold. When the shooter tries to increase the trigger pressure, extreme care should be taken to keep the correct sight alignment. Consistently accurate shots are produced when the shooter maintains intense concentration on sight alignment during the application of trigger pressure, while experiencing the minimum movement.

The target and sights cannot all be in sharp focus seeing uniformly through back sight, at the same time. It is most significant for the foresight to be in sharp focus, so that it can be accurately positioned within the framework of the back sight. If the shooter feels uncomfortable to focus on the foresight, the corrective glasses should be used. Only one eye can perceive the aim. To keep away from strain to the aiming eye the other should remain open and if one eye is shut this will try to open and a preventable strain is introduced. The best technique is to use binocular vision, but this demands schooling at an early stage. Even if the shooter does not have need of corrective glasses he/she can take

BREATHING

Breathing is one more significant constituent of a shot. While aiming breathing generates a rhythmic movement of which causes the pistol to move vertically or up and down. Therefore one must hold the breathe during the final stages of aiming and delivering a shot. The shooter should not feel over conscious of the requirement of breathing. The average individual does not generally have to think about breath and the lungs take care of the body without conscious thought. The main object of breathing is to enable the shooter to hold his breath with a relaxed feeling elongated sufficient to fire. During the breathing process, when we take a breath then exhale; there is a point where we pause breathing for a few seconds before taking the next breath. This natural and effortless state is known as respiratory pause. This pause can be prolonged for several seconds, without too much effort. The additional customary technique of breathing is to take a couple of deep breaths when prepared to pick up the pistol from the table/stand. This is to let the air to leave the lungs without feeling the strain. The duration of the respiratory pause should no be held longer than eight to twelve seconds. If the shot cannot be fired in this time, it should be cancelled and put lower the pistol, breath normally a few times, then start again.

The whole body depends on plenty of amount of oxygen to release energy from stored chemicals in the cells. To bring breathing under control the oxygen in the blood should be enhanced. For this prolonged

AIR PISTOL TARGET SHOOTING

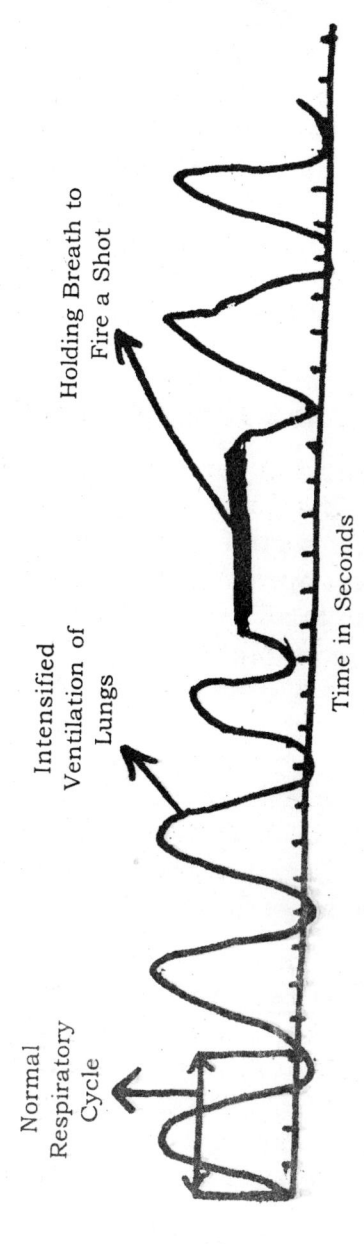

Figure 4.1 (II) : Breathing and Breath Control

breathing is necessary. The reason of controlling the breathing is to restrict the movement of the arm caused by the movement of the chest as the lungs are filled and emptied. It is predictable that the climax attempt can be sustained for about ten seconds. The skilled shooter can uphold extended time. If we hold the breath for extended time, it will enhance the pulse rate, which will cause the movement of the muzzle of the pistol in a broad and extensive arc.

TRIGGER RELEASE AND FOLLOW THROUGH

Shooting preparation comprises of getting into position, loading, holding, aiming, firing, follow through etc. However, trigger control is of utmost importance because it is the key operation in delivering a perfect shot and is common to all forms of the shooting sport. The trigger control in pistol shooting is more difficult to achieve than with the rifle because the hand must hold the pistol firmly and is thus in a state of greater muscle tone. Trigger release technique is of major and some times decisive importance in producing an accurate shot. A proper trigger release does not disturb the aim of the pistol on the target; therefore the shooter must squeeze the trigger smoothly.

Discharge of the pistol without introducing any angular misalignment between the barrel and the eye is an important feature in pistol shooting. The discharge is normally initiated by manually moving the trigger. This can be termed "trigger finger movement" and it means that simply being able to discharge the pistol without introducing angular misalignment between the

AIR PISTOL TARGET SHOOTING

barrel and the eye. In pistol shooting, learning the technique of moving trigger finger alone is the most difficult hurdle. There is one cardinal point in trigger control that when the trigger is released nothing must move but the trigger-finger and trigger. In good technique the pistol is still, properly held on perfect aim, maintained until and after the release of the shot. The application of the trigger pressure should be an uninterrupted constantly increasing positive pressure, straight to the rear. The trigger must be pressed in combination with climax visual insight, breath control, steady hold and highest concentration on the sight alignment.

With a pistol, trigger control is the essence of success and it is many times more difficult to achieve than with the rifle. It is more difficult because the hand must hold the pistol firmly and is thus in a state of greater muscle tone. Trigger release is an effort to make the trigger automatically moves smoothly when the eye determines that the sight alignment is correct. Our effort is to make this a conditional reflex and therefore the word release contributes to an erroneous.

If the trigger is fired too quickly it will be jerked and not pulled back in a smooth continues movements. A gradual increasing pressure on the trigger will coincide with the gradual improvement of the sight picture and the shot will be fired when the sight picture is held within the grouping area of the shooter. The trigger release must be in complete coordination with visual perception of the sight picture so that it occurs at that precise instant when the sights are properly aligned.

In the release technique in actual release

AIR PISTOL TARGET SHOOTING

technique, the hold is not be disturbed, eye sees the perfect picture and the trigger finger does the job of moving just as much as necessary to release.

Trigger Finger

The forefinger/trigger finger/ index finger is used only to discharge the trigger and positioned naturally on the trigger. The producing of smooth trigger action makes special demands upon the work of the right index finger when squeezing upon the trigger; its correct work determines to a great extent the quality of the shot, since the slightest incorrect movement of the finger will spoil the most careful and most delicate aim. In general only the pad of the top joint is used and this provides a good surface area.

To keep away from importing any irrelevant movement to the pistol when the trigger is released, no part of this finger must come into contact with the grip. It is important to keep the trigger finger in the same position for each shot. The trigger finger must not touch the pistol frame. Because, at the moment of trigger release, the unexpectedly relaxed muscles in the finger expand, and this could cause a slight deflection of the pistol if the finger was touching the frame. In firing the pistol, move only the pad of the trigger finger directly to the rear. This must be done with a steadily increasing pressure until the shot breaks.

AIR PISTOL TARGET SHOOTING

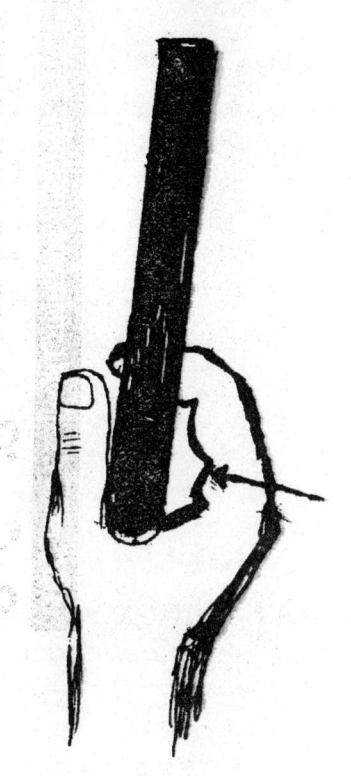

Figure 5.A.1. (II) Correct Hand and Index Finger Position

Follow through

Follow through is the effort on the part of the shooter to continue the employment of the fundamentals throughout the delivery of the shot exactly as they were planned and set-up. In follow through the air pistol keeps on aim, unmoving after the shot is released in order to avoid the early and premature relaxation in grip and focusing. In the basic training we should focus on the action of follow through until this becomes our addiction. With this short additional time we let the

AIR PISTOL TARGET SHOOTING

pellet to leave the barrel within the same circumstances.

The shooter should learn to maintain the aim and the correct sight picture, as a pistol will move a little bit because of the recoil. At this time shooter should continue motionless after this short movement and the pistol will return to its position before the release of the shot.

The above said progression should be pursued before we lose the attentiveness on the sight and relax the grip. The low velocity of the pellet and its extended barrel time necessitate the pistol to stay on aim motionless after the shot is fired. Any hasty relaxation in focusing and grip will have some bearing on the final flight-path of the pellet because of prolonged barrel time.

The positive follow through must be the part of the aiming process and must be included in fundamental training of aiming. Premature relaxation of the focus on the sights and of the grip also causes loss of control over the pistol at the firing movement. Thus follow through is an integral part of the act of aiming and it has special importance for air pistol shooting.

⬣ 3

Appended Fields
of Shooting

ANATOMY AND PHYSIOLOGY

Knowledge of the anatomical structure of the human body is necessary if the proficient application of its use is to be fully appreciated. The skeleton constitutes partly a support of compressive loads. There is a direct relationship between the degree of immobility of the pistol and accurate shooting; therefore the shooter must give serious attention to the selection of a stance, a position and the system created by the pistol and body. It is useful to know the muscles, which direct the actions of bones and joints, their location in relation to the bones and joints so that they can be identified by feel and observation.

The human skeleton is generally viewed as a passive rigid scaffold solely for protection and support. These two functions of bones are important, but bones also provide leverage for movement. The skeletal system consists of 206 bones (the numbers of bones varies slightly for the different spans of life. Their number being more during childhood as during development to maturity the separate bones fuse into single units).

It is worth examining the various anatomical components involved in the stance. The muscular and ligamental system plays an important role in the creation of stability in the shooter's stance. The passive apparatus includes the ligaments and the bones and both exert resistance. It is good and necessary for the shooter to have at least a passing knowledge of the various anatomical components involved in his/her stance.

Skeletal System

The primary organs of the skeletal system viz. bones lie buried within the muscles and other soft tissues, providing a rigid framework and supportive structure for the whole body.

In this respect the skeletal system functions like steel girders in a building. However, unlike steel girders, bones can be moved. An understanding of how bones articulate with one another in joints and how they relate to other body structures provides a basis for understanding the functions of many other organ systems. Coordinated movement for example, is possible only because of the way bones are joined to one another and their connection with muscles fibers. Bones form the body's supporting framework. Muscles are anchored firmly to bones. As muscles contract and shorten, they pull on bones and thereby move them. In the shooting stance, a static state is created by the constant isometric contractions in the opposing muscles, balancing each other out. This static state is also called a state of dynamic equilibrium.

AIR PISTOL TARGET SHOOTING

The bones are moved by muscles, which are flesh-colored fibrous structures encapsulated by fascia. If you weigh 120 pounds, about 50 pounds of your weight comes from your skeletal muscles, the "red meat" of the body that is attached to your bones. Movements caused by skeletal muscle contraction vary in complexity from holding the pistol to the coordinated and fluid movements of a gifted player. Static work of the muscles is carried out when the joints are in a certain position. The muscles are capable of remaining in this strained position for only a relatively short period of time without fatigue.

There are about 650 muscles in the body divided into three types e.g. skeletal, visceral and cardiac. In shooting we are more concerned with skeletal muscles rather than other two types. Most muscles are skeletal, and they make limb and body movement possible. Movements caused by skeletal muscle contraction vary in complexity. Nearly all are attached to bones by connective tissue known as tendons or ligaments. The nerve cells in the spinal cord keep these muscles in a state of slight tension, known as "muscle tone". They are under conscious control and are also called voluntary muscles. Skeletal muscles are made up of parallel bundles of fibers, containing thin strands of protein.

Most skeletal muscles attach to two bones that have a moveable joint between them. In other words, most muscles extend from one bone across a joint to another.

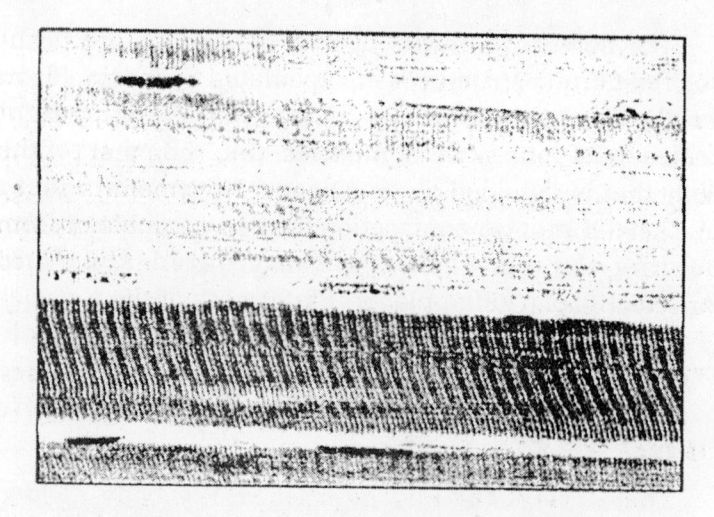

Figure 1.B.1. (III): Voluntary Muscles

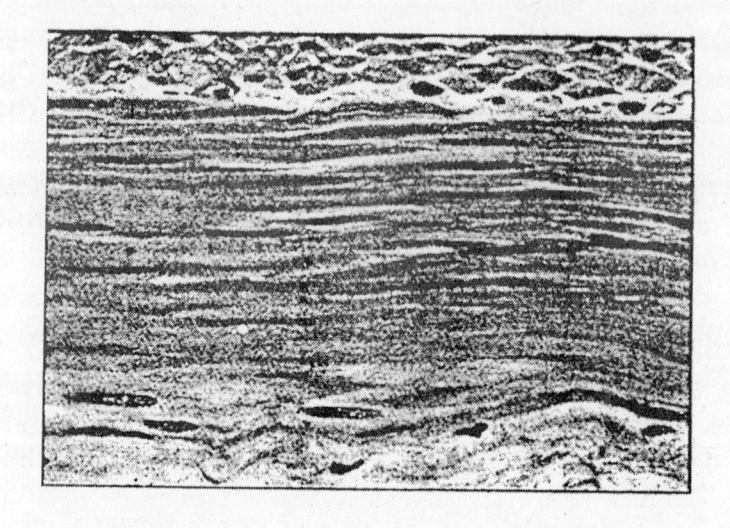

Figure 1.B.2. (III): Involuntary Muscles

AIR PISTOL TARGET SHOOTING

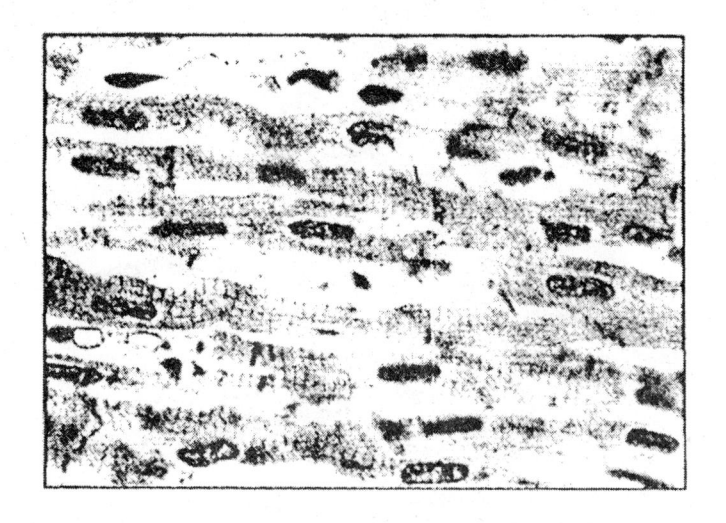

Figure 1.B.3. (III): Cardiac Muscles

Muscles move bones by pulling on them. Because the length of a skeletal muscle becomes shorter as its fibers contract, the bones to which the muscle attaches move closer. In correct shooting position many muscles of the neck are important in holding the head steady. The head contains off balance and even slight variations in the position and body-sway during aiming. During the firing stance the muscles perform static work, which leads to muscle fatigue. For this reason the shooter must allow alternating breaks between periods of assuming the firing position. This will help the muscles to regain their working ability. In addition to skeletal muscles, the body also contains two other kinds of muscle tissue. These are cardiac and visceral muscles. The visceral muscles are also known as smooth muscles, which encountered within the walls of the internal organs and play less role in assuming or maintaining a stance.

AIR PISTOL TARGET SHOOTING

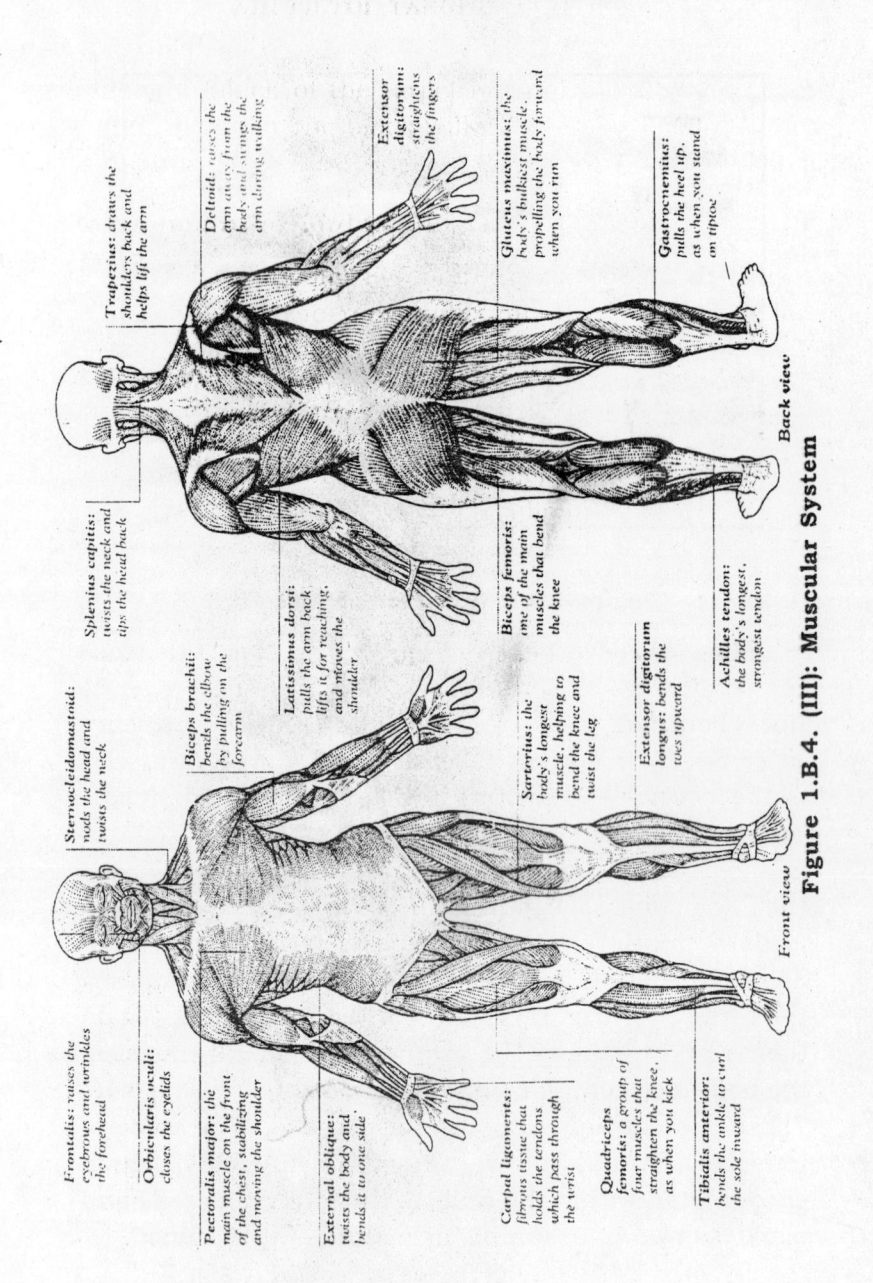

Figure 1.B.4. (III): Muscular System

Front view / *Back view*

Frontalis: raises the eyebrows and wrinkles the forehead

Orbicularis oculi: closes the eyelids

Sternocleidomastoid: nods the head and twists the neck

Pectoralis major: the main muscle on the front of the chest, stabilizing and moving the shoulder

Biceps brachii: bends the elbow by pulling on the forearm

External oblique: twists the body and bends it to one side

Carpal ligaments: fibrous tissue that holds the tendons which pass through the wrist

Quadriceps femoris: a group of four muscles that straighten the knee, as when you kick

Tibialis anterior: bends the ankle to curl the sole inward

Splenius capitis: twists the neck and tips the head back

Trapezius: draws the shoulders back and helps lift the arm

Deltoid: raises the arm away from the body and swings the arm during walking

Latissimus dorsi: pulls the arm back, lifts it for reaching, and moves the shoulder

Extensor digitorum: straightens the fingers

Sartorius: the body's longest muscle, helping to bend the knee and twist the leg

Gluteus maximus: the body's bulkiest muscle, propelling the body forward when you run

Extensor digitorum longus: bends the toes upward

Biceps femoris: one of the main muscles that bend the knee

Gastrocnemius: pulls the heel up, as when you stand on tiptoe

Achilles tendon: the body's longest, strongest tendon

AIR PISTOL TARGET SHOOTING

Muscles that move the upper extremities: The upper extremity is attached to the thorax by the fan shaped pectoralis major muscle and by the latissimus dorsi muscle. Out of these two, the former covers the upper chest and the latter takes its origin from structures over the lower back. Both muscles insert on the humorous. The pectoralis major is a flexor, and the latissimus dorsi is an extensor of the upper arm. The deltoid muscle forms the thick, rounded prominence over the shoulder and upper arm. The muscle takes its origin from the scapula and clavicle and inserts on the humerus. It is powerful abductor of the upper arm. As the name implies, the biceps brachii is a two-headed muscle that serves as a primary flexor of the forearm. It originates from the bones of the shoulder girdle and inserts on the radius in the forearm. The triceps brachii is on the posterior or back surface of the upper arm. It has three heads of origin from the shoulder girdle and inserts into the olecranon process of the ulna. The triceps is an extensor of the elbow and thus performs a straightening function. The suprasupinatus and the deltoid muscles help in raising the arm to aiming position. Holding the pistol on arm is an act against the downward force of the pistol's weight. The impulses stimulated by the weight of the pistol results in segmentary static reflexes in the muscles. The physical training can improve the strength and coordination of these muscles. The elbow joint operates on the hinge principle and it plays only passive part and is kept fully extended in the aiming position. When the elbow is extended, the biceps brachii relaxes while the triceps brachii contracts.

The correct stance is the best position that provides

a stable platform for shooter with the minimum muscular efforts. This stance provides relaxed position and balanced body without strain. This will help to reduce the excessive muscular tension, which has an adverse effect upon the nature of movement of the shooting arm. There are several types of joints e.g. ball and socket, hinge, pivot, saddle, gliding and condyloid.

Because they differ in structure, they differ also in their possible range of movement. In a ball and socket joint, a ball-shaped head of one bone fits into a concave socket of another bone. Shoulder and hip joints are example of ball-and-socket joints. Of all the joints in our bodies, these permit the widest range of movements. Due to its shape the thighbone is highly stable. The strong muscles and ligaments that surround it provide high stability. When the feet are placed at shoulder width, a very most vulnerable joint is the hip joint, but in shooting position it has passive role. Hinge joints, like the hinges on a door, allow movements in only two directions, namely, flexion and extension. Flexion is bending of a joint and extension is straightening it out. In the shooting stance the knees are fully extended because if we slightly bend them, we will lose stability. The powerful ligaments and muscles hold the complex structure of the joint during the stance position. This joint is less stable and elevated heel of the boot gives additional stability.

We stand on our feet, so certain features of their structure make them able to support the body's weight. The bones of the feet are held together in such a way as to form springy lengthwise and crosswise arches. These provide great supporting strength and a highly stable base. Strong ligaments and leg muscle tendons normally hold the foot bones firmly in their arched positions. Two arches extend in a lengthwise direction in the foot. One lies on the inside part of the foot and is called the medial longitudinal arch. The other lie along the outer edge of the foot is named the lateral longitudinal arch. Another arch extends across the ball of the foot; the transverse or metatarsal arch. These arches provide a flexible platform for supporting the weight of the body during stance. To avoid strain on any individual arch, the evenly distributed weight is recommended. The elevated heel of the shooting boot gives added stability. The backbone (vertebral-column) gives flexible yet firm support to the torso and head. The vertebral column consists of a series of separate bones or vertebrae connected in such a way that they form a flexible S shaped curved rod. The superior and inferior articular processes permit limited and controlled movement between adjacent vertebrae. The erector spinae, a mass of muscle lying behind the whole length, provide hold to the vertebral column upright. A tear in these muscle fibers can cause painful local spasm and make a correct shooting stance impossible.

The patella (kneecap) serves as the protection for the front of the knee joint when the leg is straight and as the anchor for part of the lower end of the quadriceps muscle. The kneecap acts as a fulcrum for the muscles, which straighten the leg.

Nervous System

The entire apparatus of nerve cells that controls and co-ordinates the movements of the body's internal organs and the interactions between the body and the outside world. The brain and spinal cord constitute the central nervous system (CNS) and the nerves between central nervous system and peripheral body parts make up the peripheral nervous system (PNS). To act as master organ, controlling the movements of the rest of the body, the brain need information, which is supplied by the sense organs. Acting on such information, the brain makes decisions and issues instructions. These may result in conscious actions-commanding the arm muscles to make you reach for pistol. The maintaining of equilibrium and the achieving of the greatest immobility of the body to assume firing position are important aspects of shooter's training. For this the nervous system necessarily plays an active role in the operation of muscle. The nervous system carries out its, work on the principle of reflex. Reflex action is an involuntary motor response due to a sensory stimulus or automatic conversion of an afferent stimulus into a motor effect. There are three parts of reflex arc 1. afferent limb consisting of a receptor, and an afferent nerve 2. center consisting of nerve cells where the sensory stimulus is converted into a motor impulse 3. efferent limb consisting of a motor nerve, motor endings and the effector organ. The receptor organ may be skin or sensory organ and the effector organ can be a muscle or gland.

All organs have receivers, which transmit the excitation to the central nervous system. The specialized receivers also include muscular-motor receivers, which are excited by a change in the body's stance. Therefore these receivers take part in the operation to muscular work directed at the maintaining of equilibrium and the achieving of the greatest immobility of the body.

AIR PISTOL TARGET SHOOTING

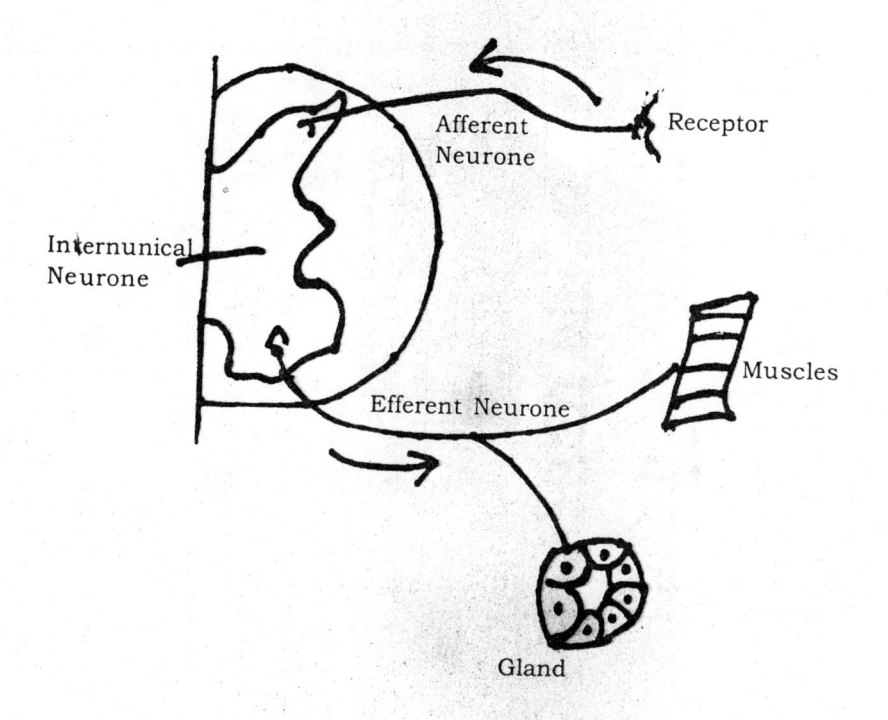

Figure 1.D.1. (III): Reflex Arc

Vestibular apparatus takes an essential part in tone, posture and equilibrium and adjusts the relative position of head to that of trunk and limbs. It also maintains the erect positions of the head and sends impulses to cortex giving information about the position (otolith organs) and rotation of head in a particular plan. It consists of bony labyrinth called membranous labyrinth. The membranous labyrinth consists of three semi-circular canals and the otolith organs, consisting of saccula and utricle. The whole structure is situated inside the vestibule. The vestibular apparatus is situated in the temporal region of the head, in the inner portion of both the ears.

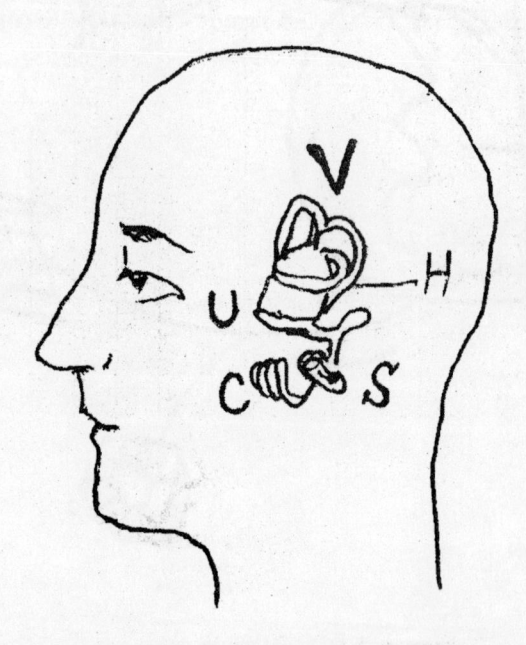

Figure 1.D.2. (III): Vestibular Apparatus

The relative position of Cochlea and vestibular apparatus on the left side.

C – Cochlea S – Saccule
H – Horizontal Canal V – Two Vertical Canal
U – Utricle

There are three semi circular canals viz. lateral, anterior (superior) and posterior. Changes in pressure of the endolymph acts as the stimulus. Since endolymph has inertia, when the head is rotated, the endolymph lags behind. Consequently, when the rotation is from

AIR PISTOL TARGET SHOOTING

left to right, pressure in the right ampulla increases, while that in the left falls. These opposite pressure changes stimulate the Crista, which send up impulses to the brain giving information about movements of the head in that plan.

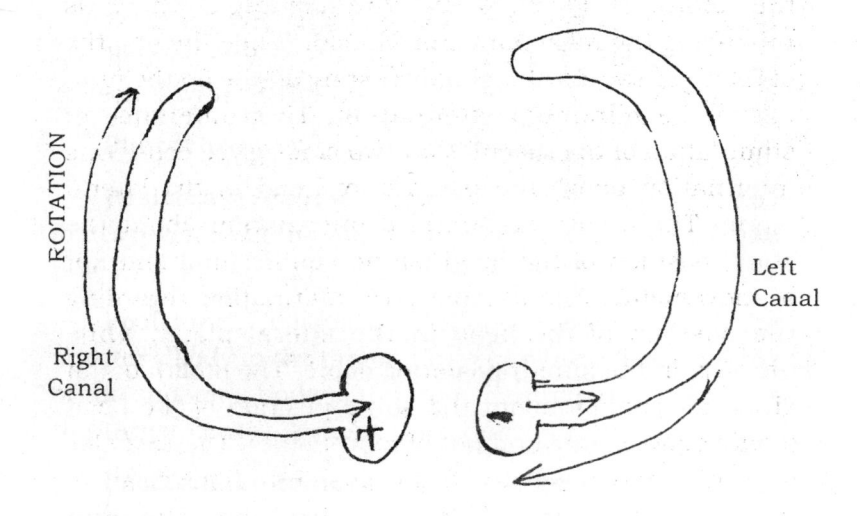

Figure 1.D.3. (III): **Mode of action of semi-circular canals.**
+ increased pressure;   − fall of pressure.

The semi circular canals give information about the direction, degree and the plane of movement of the head (kinetic or dynamic equilibrium). Each functional pair gives information and left posterior canals inform about right oblique plane, left anterior and right posterior about the left oblique plane and the two lateral canals inform about the horizontal plane. If the head movement be complex, more than one pair will come into action.

AIR PISTOL TARGET SHOOTING

The otolith organ consists of saccula, utricle and otoliths. The otolothic apparatus consists of three layers- outer coat, middle coat and inner coat. The otolith organs act as stretch receptors and gravity acts as the stimulus. When the otoliths hang down, they exert a pulling action on the hairs and produce the maximum stimulation. Consequently, when the head is tilted on the left side, the otoliths of the left saccule are handing down words producing the maximum stimulation. While the otoliths of the right saccule are simply resting on the epithelium, cause the minimum stimulation. This difference of stimulation of the saccules on two sides gives conscious information about the position of head in the lateral plane. The otolith organs give information about the static position of the head (static equilibrium) and not of movements. The saccule give information regarding the position of the head in the lateral plane, while utricles, in the antero-posterior plane. The otolith organ gives information about the static position of the head (static equilibrium) and not of movements. The saccules give information regarding the position of the head in the lateral plan, while utricles, in the antero-posterior plane.

The special nerve endings, which transmit impulses to the nervous system and constantly sending signals concerning the position of the body in space, which leads to the preservation of the particular bodily balance are also have great importance. Consequently, when the head of the shooter while assuming firing position, is held in normal position, the body will under go least amount of shifting. It is sure to make from this conclusion that the vestibular apparatus plays vital role for providing

AIR PISTOL TARGET SHOOTING

the better interrelation of the work of the skeletal musculature and it can be made appropriate which will lead the balance of the body. It is also possible to make from this important conclusion that it is not necessary to extend the head excessively towards the target or to throw the head back because this will cause strong stimulation of the receivers. Further this will create a stream of impulses, which leads to the redistribution of the tone of the skeletal musculature.

Vision

The sharpness of vision directly affect the degree of accuracy, therefore it is important that a shooter should have certain knowledge of the optical properties of the eyes. The eyes have developed from hollow outgrowths of the fore part of the brain. The adult human eye is almost spherical in shape and about 1 inch in diameter. Light reflected from objects around us enters the eyes and stimulates nerves, which feed the brain with information, which in turn interprets as visual images. The light entering the eyeball passes through the cornea, which bends it into a cone-like shaft. The iris controls the amount of light entering the eye, and the lens changes shape for near and far vision. These parts focus the light on to the area of sharpest vision i.e. yellow spot on the retina, a layer of receptors called rods and cones which convert light into nerve impulses. The receptors are connected to the optic nerve, which carries the impulses to the brain, where they are interpreted as the sensation of sight.

AIR PISTOL TARGET SHOOTING

Eyes and brain work together to analyze information and act under instructions from the brain, the eyes can select important details and eliminate irrelevant ones. The human eye cannot have a simultaneous image of objects sited at different distances, in other words it cannot focus at two different distances simultaneously. In the aiming of pistol shooting there are three objects, which are observed at the same time: the rear sight, the foresight and the target. Secondly the human eye cannot focus on a close up object and a distant object simultaneously and only one of these images will be in focus at one time. In order to obtain the correct visual perception of object, its image upon the retina must be sharp. The shooter must avoid eyestrain while aiming in vain attempts to see everything sharply at the same time. Prolonged focusing leads to rapid fatiguing of the eye muscles. Fatigue and low oxygen level will slow down the accommodation reflex, making it increasingly difficult to bring the sights into focus. Therefore the shooter must not aim for extended periods of time and in the intervals he should look into the distance in order to rest the eye muscles. It is common to find new shooters who are tense throughout a match because they attempt to maintain deep concentration. More experienced shooters generally are more relaxed between shots and when they begin a shot; they have a refined ability to narrow their concentration and can undoubtedly maintain a much deeper level of concentration during that time. Good vision care should be one of the first steps. When an individual begins a training program and it is obvious that a shooter will have correct hitting what he can see well. As the experience of shooter increases, so the perception of his vision and the visual acuity can be improved by exercise.

PHYSICAL FITNESS AND TRAINING

No sport can rely upon mental powers alone. The efficient physical application of the bones, joints, tendons and muscles of the body must also be examined, understood and applied to obtain the best performance from each individual. The mental requirements are then supported and given greater meaning, while self-confidence competitiveness and mental relaxation are also improved and developed. We need to produce a method of training to help us to control our mental and emotional process and increase our concentration whilst under conditions of competitive stress. Mental discipline is required to control the shooters actions and reactions when under competition pressures. We need to be able to overcome all hazards which require the almost exertion of a shooters mental capacity. A high degree to self control with the ability to raise ourselves above all difficulties and, at the same time, maintain presence of mind, are the qualities essential to shoot high scores in a match.

The benefits of physical fitness have become highly publicized within the past 20 years. Physical fitness is a valuable supplement to a shooting training program and an overall conditioning program is not regarded as a replacement to training on the range, but rather as an addition, to provide significant benefits with a relatively small investment of time.

There are four major benefits in relation to shooting 1) endurance for shooting training program and shooting competition 2) lungs capacity which leads to breath control 3) holding ability and 4) positive influence on the shooter's psychological stability under competitive stress results in positive mental health. Overall muscular conditioning will result in an increased ability to hold your body and a pistol stationary. A relaxed, correct position will be easier and reaction time will be faster. Aerobic conditioning will produce a more efficient cardiovascular system. The heart will be stronger, oxygen carrying capacity will be greater, and breath control will improve. The endurance gained in higher levels of fitness will make long hours of training on the range less tiring for the competitor. The most obvious cardio respiratory effect of appropriate regular exercise is an increased circulatory - respiratory capacity (aerobic power). Resting heart rate is reduced, exercise systolic blood pressure for a given exercise is reduced, stroke volume of the heart at rest (amount of blood delivered per beat) is increased, total hemoglobin, blood volume and number of red blood cells is increased, moderate hypertension (high blood pressure) is reduced and the heart can become more efficient (less oxygen required) during exercise or shooting match.

The regular exercise involving heavy ventilation (deep breathing) can increase vital capacity (functional lung volume) and maximal breathing capacity (the maximum amount of air you can move per minute).

On the surface, shooting may look as though it should not require much effort; however, the long periods of maintaining stable positions do require muscle tension. Endurance will not only make the long hours of training on the range less tiring, but will probably also make the hours more productive since there is less fatigue. The

AIR PISTOL TARGET SHOOTING

broad ranges of benefits derived from physical fitness have been recognized for years. A fitness program should be regarded as an invaluable tool and a supplement to a total shooting training program.

Since shooting is a static sports with no vigorous physical conditioning program. The stress put on shooters is significant and that the value of physical conditioning has been grossly underestimated. The shooters whose physical activities are limited to shooting acquire posture defects, spine curvature, flatfeet, forms of radiculitis (inflammation of spinal nerve roots), plexitis (inflammation of a nerve plexus), etc.

The static nature of shooting results fatigues the central nervous, muscular and support-movement system. The level of stress experienced in competition taxes the cardiovascular system and leads to fatigue. The physical condition forms the foundation of training and competition for the shooter. It increases functional abilities of the body, stimulates improvement of physical qualities and motor skills. Regular physical exercise is strongly advocates to maintain a healthy body and to ensure that a shooter has reserves of strength to compete stressful competitive matches at peak performance. There is a corresponding increase in the efficiency of the respiratory functions in order to obtain the vital oxygen so necessary for body process. This relationship is an important link in the cycle of getting oxygen into the blood stream while breath control. Physiological fitness can be attained only through exercise.

Physical training should be according the age, sex and need of the shooter. Special / specific exercises for shooting are for endurance whilst still and for achieving a good sense of balance. Additionally it is necessary to develop control over the muscles and to learn how to relax them. In weight training moderate weight and high repetitions are suggested. To achieve the endurance necessary to hold the pistol without fatigue weight can be held in position of increasingly longer period of time. To improve the balance, cycling, ballet dances, exercise on narrow beam or piece of wood or exercise on one leg are very good.

Training Program: Training is a learning process both for mind and your body and in shooting it is also donated to the time spent perfecting each element of the technique or fundamentals of shooting. To become an elite shooter, one should practice five sessions a week for about two to three hours per session. These sessions include the physical, mental, psychological and visualization techniques.

There is an old saying that "practice makes man perfect". This may be proposed "perfect practice makes man perfect". It is clear that practice makes permanent, and unless you constantly monitor and assess your training you may well be reinforcing bad habits. In training it is an important aspect to discuss the pros and cons of various techniques with fellow shooters and coaches.

A training program should be drawn up to improve or achieve the best result. Each action in the act of shooting is broken down and each part made as perfect as possible then gradually brought together. Before finalizing, it is necessary to decide what your goal may be and when you are looking for best to achieve it. A training program can be broken down into three headings: the first is physical fitness, second is specific exercises of involved body part that you may need for pistol shooting and the last is, the technical program for the increase of your shooting performance.

Mental Training

Mental discipline is required to control our mental and emotional process and increase our concentration whilst under competitive stress or pressures. Mental training is an organized and formal way learning to think about execution or performance, while practice. This is the thinking process before practice or competition about future competition. In other words, it is preparatory training about techniques to make shooter aware of his shooting process. Mental training is always considered a process of developing a positive attitude toward the achievement of your objectives.

For this we need to go through the proper mental training in our training schedule, which is required to overcome all hazards. To shoot good scores in competitive stress we need high-level concentration, self-control and stable emotions. For this the basic physical fitness, mental control and discipline and shooting training and shooting ability are major factors for consideration in training form. Positive thinking, confidence, avoidance of over confidence, continued duplication of performance and elimination of depression are major mental discipline control factors.

Strength and Isometric Training

Active movement of the skeleton is brought about by the contraction of voluntary muscles. This muscle tissue has contractile properties, which are activated by nerve impulses, to supply the effort required to move or the stabiles the body levers. Muscle work involves on increase in intra-muscular tension; when this is accompanied by a change in the length of the muscle the contraction is said to be isotonic. When intra-muscular tension is increased without a change in the length of the muscle the muscle work is isometric. There is a change in the length of a muscle when it works to produce movement in opposition to an external force. In isometric static muscle work/training the length of the muscle remains the same throughout the muscle work and no movement results. Static muscle work is more economical in pistol shooting than isotonic training, but it is fatiguing if sustained, probably because of hindrance to the circulation through the muscle.

Isometrics employ an immovable resistance and isotonic makes use of a moveable one. The word isometric itself means literally "no change/movement." An Isometric contraction is one in which the muscles contract against an immoveable resistance. The immobility of the resistance produces a tremendous amount of tension within the muscle itself. This resistance could consist of any object too heavy to move or the opposing parts of the body itself. The basic principle of isometrics is that if a muscle is contracted once a day for five seconds, at two third of its maximum power that muscle will increase significantly in strength. In a six days week this program may be conducted following two days rest. This is repeated for five weeks.

Breathing exercises should imitate these natural movements and should aim at strengthening and

AIR PISTOL TARGET SHOOTING

improving the co-ordination of all these muscles of respiration. The aim of breathing exercise should be to increase the mobility of the chest wall and the vital capacity of the lungs. In these exercises the abdominal muscles should receive attention and in particular the oblique and transversalis muscles of the abdomen. For this purpose the respiratory muscles should be exercised to the full extent of their natural range of action.

Moderate running is most effective exercise for creating demand for oxygen and the elimination of carbon dioxide. The ventilation is increased and respiratory muscles exercised and developed which improve the efficiency of the breathing apparatus. To increase the efficiency of breathing apparatus deep breathing exercises early in training programs are useful.

Dry Firing

This is a great means of reinforcing a sequence, improving trigger control and strengthening the shooting arm. In dry firing do exactly the same things you would do to live fire but don't over do dry firing. Dry firing is a great practice for teaching the body to retain constant line to the target. A black patch or target may be used as an aiming mark.

Dry firing is the act of putting an empty cartridge case in chamber, closing the bolt on it, and then applying pressure to the trigger in such a manner that the pistol fires on the empty cartridge. The purpose of dry firing is to learn to execute a trigger release so that the sights remain on the target bull during and after the trigger fires. Pistol holding is the act of holding the pistol in

AIR PISTOL TARGET SHOOTING

shooting position for extended period of time, attempting to keep the sights and target in perfect alignment. Pistol holding object is to learn to hold the sights on the target bull.

Dry shooting or training is conducted without ammunition. When a live shot is fired, some errors may be masked by the wish to achieve scores and this may spoil the technique. In dry training there is no such exterior influence to divert the attention. Dry firing develops the ability to control your shooting in all the primary factors-coordination, eyesight, arc of movement, uniformity of applying fundamentals, analysis and correction, etc. Prepare and plan each shot as if it were a live shot. A positive correction is necessary before proceeding to the next shot.

Asana: The Asana constitutes a technique in yoga which when practiced daily routine and revitalizes the whole human system. The central nervous system is the reservoir of all energy. There are latent centers in the body, which are inactive and need to be activated. The asana help this to some extent. Pranayama: Pranayama practices can help in many ways:

- To develop the respiratory organs and to improve your vital capacity (lungs capacity)
- To aid the circulation of the blood
- To produce inner, organic and natural harmony
- To provides efficient control over the respiratory movements.

- Longer and deeper breathing produces a sedative effect on nerves.

- Useful for emotional control

- Helps in steadiness of the mind and in concentration and

- More bio-energy (Prana) is absorbed and stored in the body.

Pratyahara: The psychosomatic practices of yoga bring about a state of neuromuscular relaxation and increase energy content and help the sadhaka to restrain his mind from all types of distraction, which leads to abstraction. Practices for meditation act as a quieting process so that the mind remains calm most of the time and helps you to acquire serenity of mind-a state of tranquility.

Dhyana: (Meditation): Dhyana is a branch of yoga for physical, mental and spiritual open out. Meditation for few minutes is a tonic for everyone. The practice of meditation economizes mental energies. It calms and controls the astral body. Rhythmic vibrations generated through meditation are soothing to both body and mind. It restores the vitality of the mind.

General Fitness

Good general fitness is big advantage to the competitive shooter in high pressure situations such as major competitions a healthy and fit body will handle stress more effectively. Specific warming up before a competition can be a good option, for strengthening the

AIR PISTOL TARGET SHOOTING

muscles critical for good performance.

Selecting your equipment and accessories is only the beginning. For best results, before you begin shooting, get your "shooting muscles" toned and strengthened. The physical and mental demands of shooting competition are extensive. The shooters will have a better time, i.e., shoot more accurately and be less tired, if they undergo a basic conditioning program prior to shooting. Shooting is predominately an upper-body sport; meaning that the muscles of the hands, arms, neck, back and shoulders are those taking the most stress.

Of course the benefits you will derive from any training program are relative to how you train. For example, the strength training certainly makes you stronger, but it does little to increase flexibility, so you should plan to include a variety of exercises into your overall program. To select a program, first determine your primary goals and objectives. The physically demands of a tournament are determined by (1) the type of event including length of time, distance to cover, and number of shots; (2) environmental conditions such as temperature, air and humidity; and (3) the overall fitness level of the shooter.

Begin by evaluating your present state of fitness. The basic components of physical fitness for shooting are (1) static muscular strength (2) muscular endurance; (3) respiratory fitness. Each of these components is related to both overall health and shooting performance. As you work through your exercises, be sure to work both sides of your body equally. Another thing you can do is to practice with your opposite hand. It will feel awkward at

AIR PISTOL TARGET SHOOTING

first, but keep practicing. It will get easier and you will be conditioning your left and right sides in equal amounts.

Dry practice- This exercise is similar to live shooting, only without the shots. Hold for 20 seconds; relax and gently return to its resting position. Work both sides of your body, alternating arms.

Sit Ups- Lie on the ground with knees slightly bent and feet flat on the ground. If you need extra support, put a rolled towel under the small of your back. Put your hands behind your head, elbows flat to the ground. Rise up just enough that your heads and shoulders come off the ground. While rising, elbows swing inward and point toward your knees. Return to the starting position and repeat. Be careful not to pull on your head / neck with your hands.

Flying Eagle -Stand in an open area, well away from any walls, or sit on the edge of a bench or a chair without arms. Hold your arms at your sides, and then raise them out like wings. Hold for a count to 15; slowly return to the starting position. Repeat fifteen to twenty times, which is called a "set".

There are other strengthening exercises of course, but most require access to some type of resistance-training equipment, the type of machines found in a gym. If you are interested in serious strength training, joining a gym may be your best bet. Tell the trainer that you are a shooter, and let him or her develop an exercise program for you that will enhance your shooting. On the other hand, many exercises can be done without gym so that a gym may not be necessary.

AIR PISTOL TARGET SHOOTING

Flexibility Exercises: The following are some general stretching exercises you can do at home. None require additional equipment. Be sure to wear lightweight, comfortable, clothing and well-padded athletic shoes with socks. The clothing will give you the most flexibility and good shoes will protect your bones and joints from concussion.

Upper Body Stretches

Arm Pull - Pull your left arm across your chest and rotate your head over your left shoulder. Hold for a count of 25. Now stretch your right arm and look over your right shoulder. Alternating arms, repeat 3 times.

Twist and Shout - Stand a few inches out from a wall. Place both feet facing forward and slightly bend and knees. Now, keeping your knees forward as best you can, twist your upper torso to the left and place both palms flat on the wall. Now twist to the right and place both palms flat on the wall. This is an excellent warm-up exercise that stretches both sides of your body.

Shoulder Stretch - Raise both arms over your head and interlock your fingers. Reach as high as you can, keeping you palms turned toward the ceiling. Hold for a count of 25. Stretch both sides of your truck and wrists.

Behind Your Back - Stand Up: In this exercise you will try to grasp your hands behind you back. Reach one arm over your shoulder and behind your back, and the other arm reach under your shoulder and behind your back. Repeat by alternating arm positions. This exercise stretches the shoulder and neck area.

AIR PISTOL TARGET SHOOTING

Lower Body Stretches

Groin Stretch - Sit on the floor, open your knees and bring your heels toward you. Gently hold your thighs down with your arms. Do not bounce. This stretches the inner thigh muscles.

Hip Stretch - Lie on the ground and bring the knee toward the chest, other leg extended. This stretches the hamstring muscles. Repeat this with other leg.

Bunny Hop - Balance against a wall. Stand on one leg and bend the other back. Grab your toes with your free hand and gently pull your leg up behind you. Don't pull too far. This stretches the big muscle in front of the thigh. Hold for a count of 20 and do the other leg.

To strengthen the shooting muscles a pair of 2.5 kg dumbbells can be used. Raise both arms at your side to 90 degrees and hold it for four seconds and then return to sides. This exercise may be repeated 8-10 times.

Fatigue: The fatigue can be managed to the benefit of the shooters by advance work to achieve physical and mental fitness. Fatigue affects the performance in shooting like other physical or mental activity. This is mostly resources muscle fibers, oxygen, fuel, etc. One can have high oxygen uptake due to aerobic conditioning, well tone muscle from weight training and ability to hold well due to specific and isometric training. Accumulation of lactic acid in muscle fibers and carbon dioxide in the blood can be delayed/slowdown. The ciliary muscles of eye need to be relaxed from the state of aiming as well as the directional muscles. For this we can look off into distance and back to the pistol between the shots. To manage the fatigue of leg muscles the shooter should flex the thigh and calf muscles during rest period.

The modern trend in sport is to achieve success. In this objective it is essential to train the individual in a specific manner. The concept of "specificity principle" divert attention from "unitary training" concept to highly specific training. Generally mean by "specific training" is to train the specific traits, abilities and skills required in a particular sport.

Shooting, along with other closed or open motor skill sports, relies very much on mental concentration, determination, motivation and visualization and considerable emphasis has quite rightly been placed upon the mental approach to sports training and performance. The ideal shooter should have a complete shooting technique that is simple and action should be performed smoothly and naturally, the body and pistol moving and working together as one familiar unit. The whole shooter, from head to feet, will be composed and balanced with no unnecessary tension in any area; mentally and physically relaxed, but alert.

PSYCHOLOGY IN SHOOTING SPORTS

Top performance in competitive sport can only be achieved if all the basic conditions are met optimally. Success depends not only on "external" support like training facilities, coaching or equipment but also on "internal" factors. Shooting is a learned skill that is developed through physical and psychological practice. It is the individual's desire, dedication and persistence that largely determine how successful a competitive shooter might become rather than natural ability.

AIR PISTOL TARGET SHOOTING

Psychological abilities like self-control and concentration belong to the important "internal" factors for coping successfully with the specific demands of shooting.

Sporting events with qualifying and subsequent final competitions are especially demanding as far as psychological stability is concerned, because the (top) sportsman is challenged twice in succession. The ability to keep control over mind and body is particularly crucial for success under these conditions. The shots in the finals have to be fired on command and under time pressure making it difficult for the finalist to adopt his own shooting rhythm. Nevertheless, we favor excessive emotional stimulation in the finals as the most likely cause for the decrease in performance. This is supported by the way the finals, as the decisive event, are orchestrated: commands, time limits, announcement of results and positions after every single shot increase the tension.

Moreover, a finalist is clearly separated from the rest of the competitors by being in the limelight. Spectators and competitors alike will scrutinize performance in the finals, at a time when personal initiative is restricted, closely. All these factors will certainly increase the pressure on the finalist. Interestingly, the rank of entry to the finals is of additional importance. Often this appears to determine performance in the finals to a remarkable degree. The strain seems to be particularly heavy on the favorites, who are frequently outperformed in the finals by competitors starting from lesser ranks. The latter, by contrast, face the finals rather unburdened and often perform very well.

AIR PISTOL TARGET SHOOTING

There are indications that over stimulation is the problem most frequently encountered in the finals. The psychological factors of shooting have just as much importance for a competitor as the technology behind the pistol. Successful training in competitive sports or any performance-oriented sports is based on the scientific physical and psychological, as well as technical and didactic elements required for performance. Situation dealing with psychological problems are of great importance in the shooting sports

The most common psychological symptoms in shooting are, tachycardia: increase in heart rate, hypertension: high blood pressure, tachypnoea: increased breathing rate, digestive spasms: excessive intestinal activity may cause a stomach ache or diarrhea, polyuria: frequent urination, perspiration: nervous, cold not due to heat, muscular tremors: involuntary muscular activity may cause hands shake, lack of coordination: movements may become jerky, mydriasis: enlargement of pupil of the eye, loss of the concentration, tachypsychiae: increase in speed of thought processes and vasoconstriction: lessening of blood flow to extremities.

The strategy to cope with the nervous tension is simply to accept these feelings as a normal part of competitive shooting. For the betterment of marksmanship skill realization techniques are advocated to reduce general and match tension.

Motivation

The first factor involved in learning is motivation. Before starting training the coach has to be sure that the player wants to be trained. It is initiation that makes the player act or responds to the cues presented during training. Probably the most important single variable in the acquisition of skills is motivation. If an individual is intensely interested in a given activity and is determined to do well, even to the point of sacrificing time, money and personal comfort the rate at which he learns and retains that learning is bound to be positively affected.

Motivation has been defined as the intensity of behavior relates to the degree of effort put forth to accomplish the behavior and the second aspect is direction of behavior indicates whether an individual approaches or avoids a particular situation. Thus motivation in shooting sports has a strong impact on the quality of shooter's performance. For every sport, there is an optimum arousal level, which improves performance. A shooter must have will power to over come fatigue and pain. The ability to master oneself, to force oneself to overcome difficulties and not lose confidence under any circumstances, is an important quality of character of a good shooter. Without this, no one can achieve good shooting level. A shooter must possess excellent motivational qualities, which help him to mobilize his energies for achieving victory in difficult movements of competitive pressure. For this reason the motivation training must be included in the training program of a shooter.

Concentration

The concentration is necessary for neuro-muscular co-ordination. On the other hand we can say the best concentration will give best result. The concentration is major factor in shooting sports training. The more you have the ability to attend to what you want to do the better the response and the performance. The concentration is the narrower focus of attention and for players, it represents the ability to focus on or attend to task relevant cues. The concentration is characterized by focusing on one thing at a time, focusing on present factors, selectively attending to other factors and complete involvement in the task.

Concentration is a key factor in shooting. As the shooter lifts the pistol off the bench he must concentrate hard on getting the sight picture correct, with the foresight really sharp. The optimum conditions are about five seconds, where breathing, trigger, ability to hold and concentration help for shot. But the best time to fire a shot will differ from individual to individual. The shooters need to practice concentration skills both in and off the shooting range. Like physical skill, concentration is a mental skill that must be practiced in order to gain improvement. The stance position, deep breathing, listens to body, feeling of thoughts and dry firing practice are major concentration exercises.

The acquisition of this skill requires regular, extensive and sustained practice in just the same way as do live firing in the range. Errors in aiming and performance occur when this concentration focus does not match situational demands. For concentration training four steps process is involved. The first step is observation of everything in a given environment, which is important and pertinent to our task at hand. In so doing, the extraneous information will fall to the wayside and the individual becomes aware of and comfortable with the shooting environment. His/her attention focused only to those aspects, which are appropriately focused for the challenge ahead. Second step is strategy, which involved reviewing the skill or strategies to be employed to achieve success in the imminent task demand. This will allows for short pre-performance reminder of the key elements.

The third important step is to visualize oneself performing successfully the same skills. This is to be repeated several times and at the later stage of this process not only see yourself perform, but fell it as well. Finally having observed everything, reviewed the strategies and skill, visualized and felt a successful performance, the only thing left to do is to "just do it". Trust yourself. In this step you are ready to do and skills are there, initiate the action and do it.

Relaxation

The relaxation training is beneficial to a shooter in several ways. Relaxation training allows shooters become aware of their body as well as regain a sense of control over basic psychological acts such as breathing. Secondly relaxation allows for the reduction of anxiety or over arousal by reducing the muscular tension. Third, relaxation can facilitate recovery from fatigue and injury by reducing pain associated with tension. The most important benefit is that relaxation assists in clearing the mind and assisting in concentration for physical and mental practice.

Physical exercise is an important technique for the relaxation of involved muscle groups. The progressive relaxation training for self-control needs forty minutes. The breathing exercise is second most important method of relaxation training. These exercises linked with the performance of brain and influence the activities of body cells. The respiration fuels the burning of oxygen and glucose, producing energy to power every muscular contraction, glandular secretion and mental process. The best method of breathing exercise is diaphragmatic breathing, which involves an in and out movement of the abdomen. It allows the most efficient exchange of oxygen and carbon dioxide with the least efforts. The yogic breathing, which is used to maximize inhalation & exhalation, is also a very good method for breathing & relaxation. Systematic muscular relaxation is another method used to overcome anxiety. This relaxation can be performed in several phases like; to induce tension through movement, maintaining and observing tension and experiencing relaxation. In this technique of muscular relaxation; lying on the back with closed eyes and arm drop back for the duration of 25 minutes or longer. After a short period, this exercise is repeated two to three times. Thinking positively is one way of dealing with stress, anxiety and muscular tension. It is thinking about what is good in a situation; feeling confidence and sure that something good will happen.

Attention

Correct cognitive skills such as the ability to focus and maintain attention level clear are demonstrable implications for performance. Cognitive characteristics play a major role in sport psychology. Attention is taking possession by the mind, in clear and vivid form, of one out of what seem several simultaneously possible objects.

AIR PISTOL TARGET SHOOTING

Use of the appropriate attention focus out that mental mistakes and mental mistakes often occur when a player focuses on inappropriate attention cues. Since many mistakes can be traced back to an inappropriate focus of attention coaches need to be sensitive to the attention demand and of their individual player. This will help the shooter focus on the relevant cues in the environment if coach can reduce the anxiety inherent in many learning and competitive situations.

Anxiety causes the pulse rate and blood pressure to increase, creates a poor distribution of blood, a disruption of the peristalsis in the digestive system, a widening of the windpipe and pupils and further increases the production of the sweat glands. Anxiety also causes intense nervousness, inability to concentrate, emotional instability, inability to focus and maintain attention, psychomotor restlessness, aversion to competition and no energetic fighting spirit. To over come anxiety the immersion practices in self-contemplation such as yoga, Zen Buddhism and experimental mediation is very useful. There are also methods of behavioral therapy such as autogenous training, progressive muscles relaxation, psychic desensitization and bio-feed back training.

Autogenous Training

Autogenous training consists of a system of consciously utilized psychological procedures, which help a person change to tone of his muscle system and the functioning of his psychological processes. This is a way of harmonizing psychological and physical processes. This method is used to increase the effectiveness of rehabilitation during the day, especially before training; a natural means to fight or counter act the negative consequences of long lasting emotional stress; and to alleviate the excessive emotional stress prior to a competition. This method is based on the hypothesis that every physical and psychological behavior can also be unlearned if it has been proven to be unsuitable. In shooting sport autogenous training reduces the depressive moods or physical and psychological disorders which affect the cardiovascular system, digestive system and the musculature. This technique helps us to take conscious control of excessive emotions and affections. Today autogenous training has become an essential factor for the treatment of emotional eruptions and psychic instability. Incomplete! Without experiments!

NUTRITION

The scientific analysis shows that there is a very close relationship between diet and sports performance. It is well to code here that one performs like one eats. Health and sports performance depends to a large extent on diet. Diet, in fact, is the most important factor in connection with the attainment and maintenance of health. It is a fallacy to regard that anything and everything called food is good for health. In modern sports health coupled with regulation of diet is considered a sure way to success.

Due to the high co-relation between diet and performance of person, dieticians are attached to the teams. They take into account how many calories a player consumes during exercise and decide the quantum of calories required keeping in mind the specific requirements of a player in a particular field. Dietetic propose the resume before, during and after the competition. As diet plays a significant role in the performance of a player therefore it should be handled properly. Control on eating habits especially before the competition is very necessary otherwise one's hard training would be of no use.

There is no need to have special food to shoot well but there are essentials in the diet, which make a difference. Your diet is an important part of your overall physical fitness. Eat a balanced diet, which supplies the body cells with vital nutrients in the proper proportion. All the necessary food factors like proteins, vitamins, minerals, carbohydrates and fats-are provided in the correct amounts by a balanced diet, both in term of the correct quantity and the correct type of food.

Basically, food is broken down into three forms: carbohydrates, fats and proteins. All are vital for good health, but athletes most often focus on complex carbohydrates found in such foods as potatoes, bread, lentils, vegetables, rice and nuts. In addition to the necessary starch found in these foods, they also provide all the vitamins and minerals necessary to metabolize (break down) the carbohydrates. The assimilation process is essential if the body is to utilize the nutrients found in the foods. Without it, the nutrients pass right through the body, giving little or no benefit.

Carbohydrates

Carbohydrates, provides most of our energy. Almost all foods contain some carbohydrates. The main functions of carbohydrates are to serve as an energy fuel for the body, fuel for the central nervous system and metabolism primer. Carbohydrates form the main bulk of the shooter diet and the main sources of instant energy for physical activities. Simple carbohydrates found in confectionery and processed foods provide quick energy, but offer no lasting benefits. Consumption of these foods and drinks should be kept to a minimum.

Carbohydrates are compounds of three chemical elements carbon, hydrogen and oxygen and contain no nitrogen. The plants in the sugar, starch and cellulose provide these organic compounds. Sugar is found in different varieties viz. the simple sugars, (glucose / dextrose) and fructose) and compound sugar (starch). Dextrose and fructose are found in many fruits and honey. The sugar produced from cane, maltose produced by germinating wheat and lactose found in milk are more complex. The starches and sugars are oxidized in the body through respiration and creating energy. The heat of the body and the energy required for muscular work comes from oxidation combustion or destruction of the carbohydrates.

Protein

In training period shooter needs to build up muscle strength or even to maintain it, protein is essential because these are the building blocks of our body. The shooter needs to obtain about 110 grams of protein from his/her daily diet during the training period. Proteins are constituents of all body cells and most important for the regulation of metabolic process. The primary function of proteins in bodybuilding and its repair but they also give us energy. Over 20 different kinds of amino acids are contained in various proteins. Eight of them are essential and should be present in our diet. During digestions, the proteins are broken into amino acids. These proteins obtained from milk, cheese, meat, poultry and fish are of higher value than those obtained from cereal, beans, peas and peanut. Protein is the athlete's friend. Among its many duties, protein builds and repairs muscle tissue, and every athlete wants and needs strong, healthy muscles. The best sources of protein are white meats, fish, beans, legumes, nuts and goat's milk.

Fats

Few people need to fear that they are not getting enough fat in their diet. On the whole, we should reduce the amount of fat we ingest. Some fat, of course, is essential for good health, but the amount of fat in the average diet is already excessive. Fat is beneficial because it ultimately serves as a long-range source of energy, but your primary source of fuel should be carbohydrates, not fat.

Fats like carbohydrates also consist of three chemical elements e.g. carbon, hydrogen and oxygen and contain less oxygen than carbohydrates. They are the highest form of energy producing nutrients and store energy for a long time. The Principle kinds of fats are saturated and unsaturated, which are available in the form of meat, butter and vegetable oil of mustard, coconut, seed, palm and olive oil.

Vitamins

Vitamins are essential in small amounts for our body

to regulate chemical reaction. They are essential for proper functioning of our body and to prevent deficiency diseases. Vitamins are of various type and they differ from each other in chemicals structure, physiological function and in distribution in food. Vitamins can be divided into two groups, on the basis of their solubility.

The fat-soluble vitamins can be stored in our body while others cannot. So the latter have to be added daily. Vitamins A, D, E and K are solvable in fat. Vitamins C and B are soluble in water. Fat-soluble vitamins can be stored in our bodies where as water soluble vitamins can be stored to a limited extent. The body uses these vitamins in a short period. So body has to be supplied with vitamins regularly. Excessive intake of vitamins is not advised because of their toxic effect especially fat-soluble vitamins. If vitamin deficiency remains for a long time, physical performance is affected and results in easy fatigability, muscle tenderness and less work output.

The soluble vitamin A is obtained from carrot, sweet potatoes, tomatoes, peaches, cream, butter, egg yolk and liver extracts. Sunshine is very important in producing vitamins D. Vitamins E is found in milk, butter, wheat germ and leafy vegetables. Vitamin K is available from green vegetables, soybeans and tomatoes. Vitamin C is obtained from fruits and citrus fruits are rich of vitamin C. Vitamin B is a group of nearly a dozen related vitamin and they are found together and work together in the body. They are abundantly found in milk, butter, soybean, nuts, eggs, meat, green vegetables and yeast.

Typical energy expenditure for pistol shooting is about 1.9 K calories/min or 114 K calories/hour. This amount is calculated on the basis of a 154-pound man.

AIR PISTOL TARGET SHOOTING

This would amount to 2700 K calories/day approximately. Obviously, any increased activity above resting levels will add to the projected daily expenditure.

Minerals

All food contains, besides the substances having potential energy certain saline or mineral matters. These are usually not considered food, but experience and scientific research show that their presence is absolutely necessary. There are about thirteen minerals required by the body. These are calcium, sodium, potassium, phosphorus, iron, iodine, fluorine, chlorine, copper, sulpher, zinc, manganese and magnesium. Minerals are necessary for the formation bones, growth of body cells, particularly blood corpuscles and essential ingredients in various body fluids. Minerals are abundantly found in milk, leafy vegetables, potatoes, dried fruits, meat, fish, poultry, egg and salt.

Diet before Competition

Actually there is a no food that when consumed several hours prior to training will lead to "super" performances. It does, however, require him/her to be aware of what foods will give him/her the most benefit, so that he/she can decide what, and when, to eat both before and during shooting sessions. It is throughout a year-round task. But there are certain foods that should be avoided on the day of competition, for example, fats and meats are generally digested slowly (because they require more oxygen for their oxidation). If consumed 1 to 2 hours or less before competition, they may cause a feeling of fullness, lessens the ability to concentrate, hindering performance. Other foods to be avoided are

AIR PISTOL TARGET SHOOTING

gas-forming foods, greasy foods and highly seasoned foods. These matters can be important and the shooter must decide what to eat before shooting.

Although a body cannot work efficiently on an empty stomach, neither can it perform at peak condition immediately after a heavy meal, when the oxygen required to strengthen the body and arm muscles is otherwise engaged in assisting the stomach organs in digestion. In deciding what and when to eat, therefore, the shooter must work out his requirements. If, he is to shoot soon after a meal then light food will be preferable. However when the shooter can time his shooting, it is found that a light meal, followed by a brisk walk to aid digestion, followed in turn by a short rest to relax his muscles, will give the best results. Carbohydrates should be the major constituent of the pre-competition meal and should be consumed not later than 2 and half hours before competition. Carbohydrates are easily digested and help to maintain the blood glucose levels. Increasingly popular pre-game meal is liquid meal. As both "liquid" and "meal", they contribute to hydration and to energy intake. Immediately before and during a shoot all liquid refreshments should be confined to plain water or to fruit juices. Tea and coffee are stimulants and as such should be avoided whilst stimulants may appear to be beneficial they actually cause the organs to work at a higher rate, such as faster heartbeat.

Diet during activity (replacement of sugar and water)

It is fairly common to find that athletes particularly endurance athletes, ingest glucose (usually in liquid form) during prolonged activity. It is generally agreed that ingestion of some liquid glucose during prolonged physical exercise will help spare muscle glycogen and delay or prevent hypoglycemia or low blood sugar levels. Both the glycogen sparing effect and the deterrent effect on hypoglycemia help to reduce and/or delay fatigue. It is found that ingestion of liquid glucose during long duration exercise is effective in maintaining elevated blood glucose levels, which in turn reduce fatigue during the latter part of exercise. Factors such as glycogen levels and hydration need to be tackled with the consumption of carbohydrates rich solid and liquid meals. In shorter breaks of shooting juices and carbohydrates based drinks or water may be the best choice.

Diet After Activity

Following long term exercise or training, efforts should be made to replace carbohydrates, vitamins, minerals, and water. A liquid nutrient may be consumed a few minutes following exertion in order to stabilize blood glucose. Easily digestible foods should be selected. Eating for recovery should commence as soon as the shooters can tolerate food. Early carbohydrate ingestion accelerates glycogen restoration and carbohydrate rich fluid appears to be the best recover choice for fluid and glycogen repletion.

During training the match shooter has a somewhat higher need for energy. This energy is supplied through proteins, fatty acids and carbohydrates found in diet. The right amount of food is enough. Excessive food gives no better result but can be dangerous. It is important to fuel your body before you embark on a long, tournament, but avoid excess fat and any food that is difficult to digest. After all, the purpose of your meal is to give you energy, not a stomachache. If you have additional questions about good food choices for shooters, consult your doctor. You may also find helpful information by contacting the sports medicine department of various universities.

DRUGS IN SHOOTING SPORTS

In shooting we can't attain anything with the make use of drug that cannot be skilled without them. The exercise of drugs is almost certainly the foremost trouble facing sports today. A look at the history of drug use in sports shows that drug use is not a recent phenomenon. The stimulants and drugs cause the organs to work at a higher speed than usual and should also be avoided for their advantageous life is limited. The intake of drugs is always followed by attenuation and lessening of the competence of the body as the body recuperates from the effects of the faster working rate. The drug which causes the body organs to carry out their employment at a greater rate then normal fatigues them sooner and causes them to age more rapidly.

Alcohol

Alcohol proceeds as a depressant rather than a stimulant. It agitates the vital functions like response time and reaction time, equilibrium, stability, steadiness, sense of balance, vision, precision, dull the senses, lessons the desire to win, destroys coordination and lessons the shooter's ability to concentrate. The alcohol consumption has been connected with less

AIR PISTOL TARGET SHOOTING

sensitive senses, slower reaction time, coronary heart diseases (CHD) and impaired coordination. Reactions are slowed down and concentration becomes difficult.

Stimulants

The stimulants are broad group of substances, which include caffeine, cocaine and adrenaline. Caffeine is the most widely consumed drug and it is found in coffee, tea, cola drinks and chocolates. Caffeine use is associated with increased alertness, shortened reaction time and improved concentration but there is a notable decrease in the quality of work being done. The side effects include irritability and insomnia. Caffeine raises muscular output temporarily, but in severe physical demands of longer duration, the muscular output decreases. Tea has big amounts of caffeine and tannic acid per weight, than coffee. Cola drinks contains well-known perk-up ingredient, caffeine. The side effects of use of stimulants are serious cardiovascular problems and user often shows similar behavioral changes.

Smoking

The lungs are intended to take in air from which the oxygen in abstracted, but if tobacco smoke, or indeed any other substance contaminates each inhalation, then the amount of air inhaled is decreased and an extra burden is placed on the lungs to abstract the oxygen from what is taken in. Smoking also results in a harmful coating of alveoli thereby decreasing their efficiency. With smoking nicotine, carbon monoxide, small amounts of hydrocyanic acid, pyridine and various phenols are absorbed into the lungs and mouth and our nervous system in stimulated momentarily and blood pressure goes up.

Our lungs have been taking in pure air all day and do the brain and muscles have become accustomed to receiving a ready supply of oxygen; when the oxygen becomes less accessible after contamination by the tobacco smoke the efficiency of the brain and muscles is temporarily seriously impaired until they can readjust back to what is their normal state. Carbon monoxide in the smoke fixes some of our red blood cells (RBC) so they cannot carry oxygen. Smokers also have a thicker coating of mucous in their windpipes and lungs.

FIRST AID AND CORRECTIVE LENSES

It is a good idea simply to have a first aid kit on hand and to be aware of a few steps that can be taken in an emergency. This information may be especially interesting to those engaged in field shooting where the hazards of the trail can sometimes get you, even under the best of circumstances. No doubt more people have suffered bug bites and heat stroke than any mishap with shooting tackle, per se.

First Aid Kit: It's a good idea to keep a basic first aid kit on hand at all times. Many pharmacies and sporting goods stores carry well-stocked first aid kits, but if you want to put one together yourself, the following items should be included:

- Adhesive bandages of various sizes

- Ammonia caps (for dizziness)

AIR PISTOL TARGET SHOOTING

- Antiseptic soap (for washing a wounded area)
- Antiseptic solution (for minor scrapes)
- Aspirin
- Blanket (warmth reduces chance of shock)
- Cold packs
- Elastic bandages (various sizes)
- Eyewash solution
- Gauze pads (various sizes)
- Non-stick gauze pads (for covering wounds)
- Scissors
- Tissues and pre-moistened toweled
- Tweezers (for splinters)
- Small utility knife

The phone number of the nearest ambulance service should be taped to the inside of the first aid kit. If you shoot as a club or group, all shooters should know where the first aid kit is stored and where it will be kept at all events. The best first aid kit in the world does you no good if you can't find it when you need it. When shooting at an unfamiliar location, make sure someone in your group knows the location of the closest telephone; and always keep a quarter or two in the kit so you won't have to run in circles, hunting for change in an emergency.

Care of the Eyes

Fortunately, the eye has a number of natural protective mechanisms. It is recessed in a bony socket, the quick-blinking reflexes of the eyelids and eyelashes deflect most foreign particles, and natural tears wash away most minor irritants. If you do get something in your eye, follow these simple guidelines:

Do not rub your eye or use a dirty cloth or finger to remove the foreign body. Irritants can often be eliminated by looking down and pulling the eyelid forward and down. Make sure your hands are clean. If you see a particle floating on your eye, gently remove it with a clean, sterile cloth or apply eyewash to flush the obstruction. Whatever your recreational activity, your vision plays a vital role in helping you enjoy the sport and perform at peak efficiency. Your eyes deserve the best of care.

AIR PISTOL TARGET SHOOTING

Glossary of Terms

Acclimatization: adaptation to a particular environmental stress.

Accommodation reflex: A reflex focusing action of the eye, triggered by an unclear image falling on the retina.

Accurized: Term for the careful reworking of a production action, for better grouping ability.

Action (of a pistol): The moving part, which loads the cartridge into the chamber and ejects the spent cartridge after firing.

Aerobic: in the presence of air or oxygen.

Agility: the ability to change direction rapidly while maintaining total body balance and awareness of body position.

Aiming Area: is the center area of the target as against an aiming point on the target, which is extremely difficult to attain due to the universal presence of movement in the shooter's hold.

Aiming mark: A black circular zone in the center of the target.

Aiming off: Holding your point of aim away from the centerline of the target.

Alveolar air: that air present in the alveoli which is involved in the exchange of gases with the blood in the pulmonary capillaries.

Alveoli: small air sacs, located at the termination of the pulmonary tree, in which the exchange of respiratory gases takes place with the blood in the adjacent capillaries.

Amino acids: the basic building blocks of protein.

Anabolic steroid: a prescription drug that has the anabolic or growth-stimulating characteristics of the male androgen, testosterone. Frequently taken by athletes in increase body size and muscle bulk.

Anaerobic: in the absence of oxygen.

Anemia: inadequate number of red blood cells, or low hemoglobin levels, limiting oxygen transport.

Anoxia: inadequate oxygen in the blood or tissues.

Anthropometry: the study of body measurements.

Apnoea: Suspension of breathing.

Area aiming: A method of aiming where the point of aim is maintained in an area usually below the aiming mark on the target.

ATP: adenosine triphosphate. A high-energy compound from which the body derives its energy.

Atrophy: loss of size, or mass, of body tissue, e.g., muscle atrophy with disuse.

Automatic: (a) A misnomer for self-loading semi-automatic pistols. (b) A subconscious act.

Autonomic nervous system: that portion of the nervous system that controls involuntary activity, e.g., smooth muscle and the myocardium and includes both sympathetic and parasympathetic nerves.

AIR PISTOL TARGET SHOOTING

Autonomic nervous system: The vegetative nervous system (sympathetic and parasympathetic) regulates the functioning of internal organs. It is not under the direct control of the brain.

Ball and Dummy: is a training exercise wherein the shooter makes an effort to employ all the control factors for firing a good shot. The ammunition inserted into the pistol by the coach is a random selection of live or dummy ammunition. The training aids the shooter in overcoming reaction to the recoil and loud noise of firing, preventing uncontrolled reflexes from disturbing the hold, and perfecting sight alignment.

Blood pressure: the force that blood exerts against the walls of the vessels or heart.

Body awareness: The ability to recognize the precise positional interrelation of various parts of the body (in particular in the stance, grip and aim) and the ability to reproduce the same position when required.

Bore: The inside of a barrel, which can be smooth or rifled.

Breath Control: is the ability to temporarily suspend breathing while firing a shot without being conscious of the need to take another breath. This awareness disturbs the shooter's concentration on maintaining perfect sight alignment.

Caliber: The interior diameter of the barrel. 'Small-bore' refers to a caliber of .22 in, (5.6 mm). 'Full-bore' refers to a caliber of .30 in (7.62 mm) or over.

Calling (a shot): The ability to estimate the position of a hit on the target, by recalling precisely the position of the sights at the very moment the shot was released.

Calorie: a unit of heart energy defined as the amount of heat required to raise the temperature of one kilogram of water 1o C, from 15 to 16o C.

Cant: Holding the pistol in such a manner that the sights are at an angle to the horizontal.

Carbohydrate: a food substance that includes various sugars and starches and is found in the body in the form of glucose and glycogen.

Cardiac muscle: the myocardium, or muscle, of the heart

Cardiac output: output, or volume, of blood pumped by the heart per minute or the product of heart rate and stroke volume.

Catabolism: the tearing down, or destruction, of body tissue.

Center aim: Aiming the pistol so that the sights are lined up on the center of the aiming mark.

Central nervous system: that division of the nervous system that includes the brain and spinal cord.

Cerebellum: the hindbrain, responsible for the smooth coordination of body movements.

Cerebral cortex: the portion of the brain that contains the primary and supplementary patterns of a voluntary nature.

Cholesterol: a lipid or fatty substance essential for life and found in various tissues and fluids. Elevated levels in the blood have been associated with an

AIR PISTOL TARGET SHOOTING

increased risk of cardiovascular disease.

Circuit training: selected exercise or activities performed in sequence, as rapidly as possible.

Competition trigger: A trigger specially designed for competition use, giving a greater degree of control and consistency. Examples: wider trigger, angled trigger, button trigger, extended trigger etc.

Concentric contraction: a muscular contraction in which shortening of the muscle occurs.

Conditioned reflex: a nervous reflex pattern that is learned.

Conscious firing: When the shot is released by a deliberate action of pulling the trigger.

Coordination: the act of movement in an organized, controlled, and precise manner.

Course of fire: The particular conditions of each competition, specifying the number of shot, the distance and time limits.

Crimp: The extreme edge of the cartridge case where it is bent inward to grip the bullet tightly.

Diaphragm (a) Anatomical: The muscle dividing the chest and abdominal cavities; the main muscle used for breathing. (b) Orthoptic: A circular eyepiece in which the size of the central aperture and hence the amount of light admitted through it can be varied.

Diastolic pressure: the lowest pressure of the arterial blood against the walls of the vessels or heart resulting from the diastole of the heart.

AIR PISTOL TARGET SHOOTING

Diuretic: a substance that increases kidney function leading to a loss of body fluids through frequent urination.

Dominant eye: The eye, which centers on an object in binocular vision, dominating the other eye. This is the eye usually used for sighting.

Doubling: Firing a second shot while the pistol remains on aim.

Dry Firing: is a training exercise wherein the shooter employs all the factors of controlling the firing of an accurate shot without using live ammunication.

Dyspnea: labored breathing.

Eccentric contraction: lengthening of the muscle under tension, as when lowering a heavy object.

Effective blood volume: that volume of blood available to supply the exercising muscles.

Electromyography: A measurement of muscle activity by electronic means.

Endurance: the ability to resist fatigue. Includes muscular endurance, which is a local or specific endurance, and cardiovascular endurance, which is more general, total body endurance.

Ergogenic aid: substance or phenomenon that elevates or improves physical performance.

Fartlek training: speed play, where the athlete varies his pace at will from fast sprints to slow jogging; normally performed in the country, using hills.

Fast rise: A method of bringing the pistol on aim.

AIR PISTOL TARGET SHOOTING

Fat: a food substance that is composed of glycerol and fatty acids.

Fatigue: inability to continue work, due to any one or a combination of factors.

Firing pin : Part of the hammer, or part activated by the hammer, which detonates the primer of the cartridge by striking it.

Firing Point: An area from which the shooter may address the target.

Flexibility: the range of movement of a specific joint or a group of joints, influenced by the associated bones and bony structures, muscles, tendons, and ligaments.

Follow Through: is the effort on the part of the shooter to continue the employment of the fundamentals throughout the deliver of the shot exactly as they were planned and set-up.

Glucose: a simple sugar, which is transported in the blood and metabolized in the tissues.

Glycogen: the storage form of carbohydrates in the body, found predominantly in the muscles and liver.

Grip: of the shooting hand on the pistol provides the shooter with a firm hold on the weapon that prevents shifting during recoil and a natural alignment of the sights without moving the head or wrist from their normal attitudes.

Group: A group of shots on the target: its size, shape and position each is significant.

Hemoglobin: iron pigment of the red blood cell that has a high affinity for oxygen.

AIR PISTOL TARGET SHOOTING

Hormone: a chemical substance produced or released by one of the endocrine glands, which is transported by the blood to a specific target organ.

Hypertension: abnormally high blood pressure, usually defined in adults as a systolic pressure in excess of 140 mmHg and/or diastolic pressure in excess of 90 mmHg.

Hypertrophy: increase in the size, or mass, of an organ or body tissue.

Hyperventilation: breathing rate and/or tidal volume increased above levels necessary for normal function.

Hypotension: an abnormally low blood pressure.

Hypoxia: Low oxygen level in the blood or in body tissues.

In-line stance: A stance in which both feet of the shooter are placed on an imaginary line at 90 degrees to the target.

Internal respiration: the exchange of gases between the blood and tissues.

Internal training: training program that alternates bouts of heavy or very heavy work with periods of rest or light work.

Ischemia: Oxygen starvation of (muscle) tissue.

Isokinetic contraction: contraction in which the muscle generates force against a variable resistance.

Isometric contraction: contraction in which the muscle generates force, but there is no observable

AIR PISTOL TARGET SHOOTING

movement, e.g., pushing against a building.

Isometric: Of equal measure. In isometric excercises (at the isometric bar) the muscle fibres contract equally.

Isotonic: Of equal tension. In isotonic excercises (with an elastic strap) the muscle fibres are similarly tensed when raising or lowering the arm.

Jerking: A faulty action of operating the trigger.

Kinesthesis: a sense, or awareness, of body position.

Lactic acid: the end product of glycolysis, or anaerobic metabolism.

Latency period: The time elapsing between the arrival of a nerve impulse at a muscle and the commencement of the muscle contraction.

Lipid: fat, or fat-like, substance.

Lock time: The time elapsing between the activating of the trigger and the detonation of the primer of the cartridge.

Magazine: A part of semi-automatic pistols, containing the cartridges, which are fed into the action by the magazine spring.

Maximal oxygen uptake (VO_2 max): the best physiological index of total body endurance. Also referred to as aerobic power, maximal oxygen intake, maximal oxygen consumption, and cardiovascular endurance capacity.

Mental Discipline: in pistol marksmanship is the shooter's ability to maintain his concentration on sight alignment while the other fundamentals of minimum arc of movement and trigger control are being employed at their optimum.

Mental rehearsal: A form of mental training in which parts of the shooting technique are learned by repetitive consideration.

Metabolism: the sum total of the energy-producing and -absorbing process in the body, i.e., the energy used by the body.

Minimum Arc of Movement: is the smallest degree of movement that the shooter can attain in the body. Shooting arm and weapon during the time of firing a shot.

Muscle tone: The continues slight tension of skeletal muscles present even at rest.

Muzzle flick: A movement of the muzzle as a consequence of faulty trigger release.

Muzzle: Open end of the barrel.

Muzzle-brake: An attachment to the muzzle designed to vent some of the propellant gases at an angle so that the recoil is reduced.

Neuron: the nerve cell; the basic structural unit of the nervous system. Conducts nervous impulses to and from various parts of the body.

Open stance: A stance in which the shooter is chest on to the target.

Optimum period: A period during which the shot should be released.

Orthoptics: Optical devices such as shooting glasses,

AIR PISTOL TARGET SHOOTING

tinted lenses, adjustable diaphragms etc.

Oxygen debt: the quantity of oxygen above normal resting levels used in the period of recovery from any specific exercise or muscular activity.

Pellet Catcher: A simple box placed in back of target paper, which has within it a vertical or inclined metal plate. On impact with the plate the pellets lose virtually all their energy in deformation and the remnants are collected with in the box.

Photochromic: Light and color sensitivity.

Position sensors: Sensitive nerve endings in the joints registering the minute position change which take place.

Position: of a pistol shooter is the relationship of the shooter's body to the target. Proper or natural positioning of the shooter's body points the shooting arm directly at the target center without deviation.

Positional memory: Ability to reproduce certain positions in the stance, aim and in the placing of the trigger finger. See also under body awareness.

Positive Pressure: Pressure on the trigger, which is an uninterrupted, constantly increasing pressure applied by the trigger finger in an effort to fire the shot. This pressure is initiated by the presence of a satisfactory minimum are of movement in conjunction with perfect sight alignment, not perfect sight picture. A perfect sight picture is the absence of movement combined with perfect sight alignment.

Power: the product of force and velocity. This is probably far more important than absolute strength

AIR PISTOL TARGET SHOOTING

alone.

Primer: Sensitive explosive substance which ignites the main charge of the cartridge.

Progressive resistance exercise (PRW): the resistance used in training is progressively increased systematically as the body adapts to the training stimulus.

Prone: Laying face downwards. (Compare supine).

Protein: a food substance formed from amino acids.

Prove: To show that a firearm is unloaded and hence safe.

Proving range: A range area set aside to the test the functioning of pistols.

Pushing/pulling (the trigger): Incorrect technique of trigger release.

Quadrant timing: A method of practicing fast and smooth trigger release.

Reaction time: the period of time between the presentation of a stimulus and the subsequent reaction to that stimulus.

Ready position: In all 25 meters timed event, shooting starts from this position: the shooter's arm holding the pistol must point downwards at an angle of not greater than 45 degrees from the vertical, until the targets begin to face.

Residual volume: that volume of air remaining in the lung following a maximal expiration. Vital capacity plus residual volume equal total lung capacity.

AIR PISTOL TARGET SHOOTING

Respiration: the exchange of gases at both the level of the lung and tissue.

Retina: Light sensitive layer at the back of the eye.

Rollover trigger: A trigger action where there is a smooth gradual movement of the trigger leading to the release of the shot.

Score index: A training score recorded to indicate progress.

Second pressure: Increasing the initial pressure applied to the trigger while one aim.

Segmentary static reflex: A reflex action by which segments of muscles maintain tension in turn against the pull of gravity (when holding a pistol on aim, for example).

Semi-automatic: An action of a pistol where one shot only is released by each activation of the trigger.

Sensory nerve: afferent or sensory nerves transmit impulses from the sensory organs to the central nervous system.

Set trigger: A trigger mechanism where there are essentially two triggers: a primary trigger, which requires much less force to operate, releases the main trigger.

Sight Alignment: is the relationship of the front sight to the notch of the rear sight as seen by the shooter's eye. The top of the front sight must be level with the level with the top of the rear sight and the light space must be equal on each side for the front sight.

Sight picture: The visualization of the sights and

the aiming mark on the target.

Sight ratio: the relative sizes of the front sight and the rear sight notch.

Six o' clock aim: Aiming the pistol so that the sights are lined up immediately below the aiming mark on the target.

Skeletal muscle: muscle controlling skeletal movement that is normally under voluntary control.

Slow-rise: A method of bringing the pistol on aim.

Stance: The interrelated position of the feet, torso and heat when addressing the target.

Step shooting: A form of training where the shooter gives himself increasingly more difficult goals to achieve.

Stocks: The part of the pistol by which it is gripped by the shooter's hand. Usually made out of wood and shaped to the contours of the hand.

Strength: the ability of a muscle to exert force.

Stroke volume (of the heart): The amount of blood pumped out by the heart with a single contraction (beat).

Subconscious firing: When the shot is released without a conscious effort on the part of the shooter.

The Fundamentals of Pistol Marksmanship: are those essential factors that the shooter must know and learn to control in order to fire an accurate shot.

Tidal volume: the amount of air inspired or expired during a normal breathing cycle.

Training games: A method of training practiced by

AIR PISTOL TARGET SHOOTING

two or more shooters in which a strong competitive element is engendered.

Trigger Control: is the ability of the pistol shooter to apply pressure on the trigger to fire the weapon without disturbing sight alignment.

Trigger Shoe: A metal or plastic sleeve which, when fitted on the trigger, alters its shape, angle or position, allowing greater control.

Trigger Shyness: A mental block, which inhibits the shooter from releasing the shot, even though conditions are favorable.

Trigger: The part of the pistol, which activates the 'sear', thus allowing the hammer to fall and detonate the primer of the cartridge.

Ventilation: movement of air into and out of the lung.

Vertical rise: A method of bringing the pistol into the aiming position.

Visual hallucination: Retained images on the retina by over stimulation of the visual receptors.

Vital capacity (of the lungs): the volume of air, which can be expelled from the lungs after the deepest possible inspiration. (Average for a health adult is 3.8 liters.)

Wadcutter ammunition: Ammunition in which the bullet has an almost flat face, and hence cuts a clear punched-out hole in the target.

Zeroing: is the technique of setting your sights so that a shot called good, (undisturbed perfect sight alignment and minimum are of movement) will hit the center of the target on an ideal day with no wind. This is an exercise by which the shooter brings the center of his (shot) group to the center of the target by adjusting the sights on his pistol.

References

Antal, Laslo (1989) Competitive Pistol Shooting, London, A&C Black Publishers.

Barnett, M.L. and Stanicek, J.A. (1979), Effects of Goal Setting on Achievement in Archery, *Research Quarterly*, 50 (3), 328-322.

Benson, H. (1975) The Relaxation Response, New York, William Morrow.

Bernstein, D., and Borkovec. T. (1973) Progressive Relaxation Training, Champaign, IL: Research Press.

Blair, Wesley (1984) The Complete Book of Target Shooting, Harrisburg, Stackpole Books Publishers.

Blenda, P.R. (1979) Simulating Various Levels of Darkness with Light Attenuating Devices (LAD's) Human Factors, 21(5), 605-610.

Buss, A., Booker, A., and Buss, E. (1972) Firing a Weapon and Aggression. *Journal of Personality and Social Psychology*, 22 (3), 296-302.

Cartner, J.A., and Tierney, T.J. Jr. (1978) Sex Differences in Prediction of Confidence in Marksmanship Performance, Perceptual and Motor Skills, 46, 207-210.

Cheetham, P.J. (1982) Biomechanics Research Studies in Shooting Sports using the Selspot II System,

Unpublished Manuscript, Colorado Springs, United States Olympic Committee, Olympic Complex.

Cheethan, D., and Landers, D. (1982) A Cinematographical Analysis of Rapid Fire Pistol Shooting and Running Game Target Shooting, Unpublished Manuscript, Tempe, Arizona State University.

Christinia, R.W., and Lambert, A.L. (1984) Development of a Portable, Low-Cost Prototype Instructional Shooting Simulator to Improve Rifle and Pistol Shooting Performance of Subelite and Elite Competitors. Final Research Report (GIA 83-25) University Park, PA: Pennsylvania State University, Motor Behaviour Laboratory.

Coleman, J.A. (1978) Psychology and Shooting, *Journal of International Shooting Sport*, 1(2), 67-68; 70-72; 74.

Coleman, J.A. (1980) Personality and Stress in the Shooting Sports, *Journal of Psychosomatic Research*, 24; 287-296.

Daniels, F. and Landers, D. (1981) Do the Eyes have it? American Rifleman, pp. 38-39, 70.

Davis, S., Hersh, L., and Nevitt, J. (1976) Behaviour Shaping Techniques and Personalized Instruction in an Archery Class, *Perceptual and Motor Skills*, 43, 913-914.

Dillman, C.J. Cheetham, P.J. and Bauer, S.J. (1984) Body Stability Analysis of Rifle Shooting, Unpublished Manuscript, Colorado Springs,

CO, Department of Biomechanics and Computer Services, Sports Medicine Division.

Doyle, L. (1981) *Difference Effectiveness of Relaxation Procedures in Attenuating Components of Anxiety in Shooters, Unpublished* master's Thesis, Pennsylvania, Pennsylvania State University.

Easley, D., Wright, D., Warnick, W., and Gipe (1969) The Effects of Interruption of Dark Adaptation on Performance of Two Military Tasks at Night, Human Resources Research Organization, Technical Report, 69-20.

Etzel, E., Jr. (1979). Validation of a Conceptual Model Characterizing Attention Among International Rifle Shooters, *Journal of Sport Psychology*, 1, 281-290.

Farness, M. (1994). Target Shooting, New York, KTG Publisher.

Froberg, J. (1974) Circadian Rhythms in Catecholamine Excretion, Performance and Self-Ratings, Reports from *The Laboratory for Clinical Stress Research*, No. 36, Departments of Medicine and Psychiatry, Stockholm.

Gregg, J.R. (1980) How to Prescribe for Hunters and Marksmen, *Journal of the American Optometric Association*, 51(17), 675-680.

Hall, E.G. (1983) *Ready, Aim, Fire ..... The Efficacy of Transcendental Medication and Progressive Relaxation with Imagery for Enhancing Pistol Marksmanship.* University, Baton Rouge, LA 70803.

Halnau, Clive R.E. (1986) Shooting Sport Technique and Practice, Bisley, Casiberra Publishers.

Hartink, A.E. (2004) The Complete Encyclopaedia of Rifle and Carbines, Groningen, Rebo Publishers.

Hatfield, B.D., Landers, D.M. Ray, W.J. and Daniels, F.S. (1982) An Electro-encephalographic Study of Elite Rifle Shooters, *American Marksman*, pp. 6-8.

Hatfield, B.O., Landers, D.M., and Ray, W.J. (1984) Cognitive Processes during Self-Paced Motor Performance: An Electroencephalographic Profile of Skilled Marksmen, *Journal of Sport Psychology*, 6(1), 42-59.

Haywood, K.M. (1979) Skill Performance on Biorhythm Theory's Physically Critical Day, *Perceptual and Motor Skills*, 48, 373-374.

Henderson, S.E. (1975) Predicting the Accuracy of a Throw without Visual Feedback, *Journal of Human Movement Studies*, 1, 183-189.

Herrigel, Eugen (1953) Zen and the Art of Archery, Routledge and Kegan, Paul Publication.

Hickey, Bob and Sievers, Art (1996) Successful Pistol Shooting, Tucson, STP Books.

Hinchliffe, K.B. (1981) Target Pistol Shooting, London, David and Charles Publishers.

Jones, Jr., R.S. (1978) Rifle Accuracy as a Function of Electrodermal Activity, Cookeville, Unpublished Master's Thesis, Tennessec Technological University.

Keller, F.S. (1968) "Good-bye Teacher ...." *Journal of Applied Behaviour Analysis*, 1, 79-89.

Keller, F.S. (1969) A Programmed System of Instruction, *Educational Technology Monographs*, 2, No. 1.

Krahenbuhl, G. and Harris, J. (1985) *Biochemical Response Profile of Elite Shooters,* Copenhagen, Paper Presented at the VI World Congress in Sports Psychology.

Kratzer, H. (1982) Pulling the Trigger: Some Remarks on its Psychical Regulation, *Journal of International Shooting Union 1, 3,* 17, 31, 33, 35, 37, (the English Version of the Article is printed on pp. 17 and 31).

Krilling, William (1986) Shooting for Gold, Georgia Notional Rifle Association U.S.A.

Landers, D.M., Christina, R. Hatfield, B. Daniels, F. and Doyle, D. (1980) Moving Competitive Shooting into the Scientist's Lab. American Rifleman, pp. 36-38.

Landers, D.M., Daniels, F.S. (1988) Shooting Sports Research, Washington, National Rifle Association of America.

Landers, D.M., Daniels, F.S., Hatfield, B.D., and Wilkinson, M.D. (1982) Respiration, Shot, Head, *Journal of International Shooting Union,* 24, 21-23, 27, 28.

Landers, D.M., Wang and Courtet (1985) Peripheral Narrowing Among Experienced and Inexperienced Rifle Shooters Under Low and

High Stress Conditions, *Research Quarterly for Exercise and Sport*, 52(2), 122-130.

Lehrl, V., Blaha, S. and Sporl, G. (1977) Psychic Condition of Marksman in Training with Placebo and Oxprenolol, Sportarzt and Sportmedizin, 28(3), 86-93.

Marshall, A., Bond, G., Shaw, B., Purvis, E., and Fields, R. (1987) Artificial Intelligence/Expert System (M-16A1 Rifle), Unpublished Manuscript, A.H. Marshall, Orlando, Naval Training Equipment Centre.

McGrath, J. (1962) The Influence of Positive Interpersonal Relations on Adjustment on Effectiveness in Rifle Teams, *Journal of Abnormal and Social Psychology*. 65(5), 365-375.

Meyer, W., Folkers, V. and Weiner, B. (1976) The Perceived Informational Value and Affective Consequences of Choice Behaviour on Intermediate Difficulty Task Selection, *Journal of Research Personality.* 10. 410-423.

Monters, J.I., (1975) Psychological Preparation on the Shooter, *Journal of International Shooting Union*, 15(5), 18-22.

Moscu, I. (1972) Experimental Investigations on the Emotively of Top Sportsmen, *Revue Roumaine des Sciences Sociales: Serie de Psychologie*, 16(1), 29-40.

Myers, A. (1962) Team Competition, Success and the Adjustment of Group Members, *Journal of Abnormal and Social Psychology*, 65(5), 325-332.

Ninima, V., McAvoy, T. (1983) Influence of Exercise on Body Sway in the Standing Rifle Shooting Position, *Canadian Journal of Applied Sport Sciences,* 8(1), 30-33.

Palmblad, J. Blomback, M. Egberg, N., Froberg, J., Karlsson, C., and Levi, L. (1975) Experimentally Induced Stress in Man: Effects on Blood Coagulation and Fibrinolysis, *Reports from the Laboratory for Clinical Stress Research.* No. 42, Stockholm, Departments of Medicine and Psychiatry.

Palmblrad, J. Froberg, J. Granstrom, M. Karlsson, A. Levi, L. and Unger, P. (1973) Stress and the Human Granulocyte: Phagocytosis and Turnover, *Reports from the Laboratory for Clinical Stress Research.* No. 34, Stockholm, Departments of Medicine and Psychiatry.

Parish, David (1997) Successful Rifle Shooting, Marlborough, The Crowood Press.

Porac, C. and Coren, S. (1981) Lateral Preferences and Human Behaviour (pp. 188-213) New York, Springer-Verlag.

Pullam, B. (1973) Position Rifle Shooting, Winchester, United States Marksmanship.

Reynolds, Mike (1988) Shooting Made Easy, Ramsbury, The Crowood Press.

Rigby, W.R. (1980) Personality Characteristics of United States International Rifle Shooters, Maryland, Unpublished Doctoral Dissertation.

Ripoll, H., Papin, J., Guezennec, J., Verdy, J., and Philip

M. (1985) Analysis of Visual Scanning Patterns of Pistol Shooters — Speed Shooting in Dueling Pistol, In: D. Landers (Ed.), Sport and Elite Performers. Champaign, IL: Human Kinetics.

Rotter, J.B. (1954) Social Learning and Clinical Psychology, New York, Prentice-Hall.

Runninger, J. (1980) "Eyes on the Ball," An Oversimplification, *Journal of the American Optometric Associations,* 5(7), 667-670.

Schwartz, J.C., Gold, G. and Seeman, G. (1970) A Comparison of Massed and Spaced Extinction of Expectancies for Success, *Journal of Experimental Research in Personality,* 4, 129-134.

Shelamov, B. and Bablin V. (1982) Physical Fitness as a Determining Factor of Reserve Abilities of a Top Level Sport Shooter, Proceedings of the Second Scientific Congress in Sport Shooting, 107-112.

Sherman, A., (1980) Overview of Research Information Regarding Vision and Sports, *Journal of the American Optometric Association,* 51 (7), 661-666.

Singh, Karni (1982) From Rome to Moscow, Bikaner, Munshiram Manoharlal Publishers.

Starkers, J.L. and Lafreniere, P.D. (1982) Anticipatory Behaviour in Rifle Shooters, Paper presented at the Canadian Society for Psychomotor Learning and Sport Psychology.

Starkersm J.L. (1982) Report to the Shooting Federation

of Canada, Unpublished Manuscript, Ontario, McMaster University.

Stine, C., Arterburn, M. and Stern N. (1982) Vision and Sports: A Review of the Literature, *Journal of the American Optometric Association*, 53(8), 627-633.

Teitge, D.W. (1983) Minding the Team: A Median Approach to Competitive Team Coaching, *International Review of Sport Sociology.* 18 (2), 83-98.

Tieg, D. (1980) Sports Vision Care: The Eyes have it!, *Journal of the American Optometric Association,* 51(7), 671-674.

Tierney, T.J., Jr., Cartner, J.A. and Thompson, T.J., (1979) Basic Rifle Marksmanship Test: Trainee Pretest and Posttest Attitudes. (Technical Paper 354) Fort Benning, GA: U.S. Army Research Institute for the Behavioural and Social Sciences.

Tretilova, T.A. and Rodmiki, E.M. (1979) Investigation of the Emotional State of Rifle Shooters, *Theory and Practical of Physical Culture,* 5, 28.

U.S. Army Marksmanship Unit (1978) International Rifle Marksmanship Guide, Washington, D.C.: U.S. Government Printing Office.

Willis, M.P. (1967) Stress Effects on Skill, *Journal of Experimental Psychology,* 74(4), 460-465.

Yur'yev, A.A. (1973) Competitive Shooting, Washington, National Rifle Association Publications.